Cooking with Crème Fraîche

MARTINE BOUTRON
EDITED BY ANNE AGER
PHOTOGRAPHY BY ALAIN LECHAT

CASSELL

Publisher's note:
METRIC AND IMPERIAL MEASURES
The recipes in this book list ingredients in both metric and imperial measures. For best results cooks should follow **either** metric **or** imperial measures for any recipe.

Typeset by Litho Link Ltd, Welshpool, Powys, Wales.

Printed and bound in Portugal, by Printer Portuguesa-Sintra

CONTENTS

La Crème de la Crème

Or, more particularly, LA CRÈME FRAÎCHE . . . the cream that no cook, amateur or professional, British or French, can do without!

I have had a love affair with France for many years . . . a love affair that embraces not only the country, the people and the traditions, but also, most of all, its cuisine. And it started at an early and impressionable age.

Whilst training as a young chef, I soon learned the importance of first-class ingredients and the clever 'marriage' of different elements that go into making a complete dish, the most acclaimed of which was invariably the sauce.

It is the elements of a good sauce that have stayed with me, throughout my cooking and writing career, on both sides of the Channel. The secret of a great sauce is often largely due to its texture: 'une consistance oncteuse', three words which wonderfully describe the satin-like qualities of a truly excellent sauce. And how is this touch of culinary magic achieved? . . . With the addition of crème fraîche.

I was therefore delighted to be asked by Yoplait to translate this book: a 'work cocktail' that would encompass my love for France, fine cuisine and, one of my favourite food ingredients, crème fraîche.

The recipes in the book are many and varied and not all are for a sauce! I hope that you enjoy trying them as much as I have enjoyed adapting them to a British kitchen. I agree with the sentiment of Chef Georges Blanc, who wrote the foreword to the French edition, 'There is no great cuisine without cream . . . especially crème fraîche!'

ANNE AGER

The Natural Cream

Cream has been highly prized by many nationalities over the centuries, from the early culinary efforts of the Vikings and Celts, to the peoples of modern-day Europe. In France, and in many other European countries, it is responsible for the richness and delicacy of a wide variety of dishes, both for special occasions and for everyday.

Cream is a traditional product as well as a natural one. A great deal of care and attention to detail is needed in its production. The quality and purity of crème fraîche, combined with its other individual characteristics, make it an ideal ingredient for the European cuisine of today . . . healthy, light and very versatile.

Crème Fraîche: Dairy Technology at its Finest

On farms, cream is usually produced in a very simplistic manner. Fresh milk is left to stand for several hours until a thick layer of sweetly aromatic cream forms on the surface. In country regions in France, this 'farm cream' finds its way on to the top of cakes and gâteaux, and is frequently stirred into the large cups of strong breakfast coffee.

On a commercial scale, the milk fats that go into making cream are collected by a series of highly controlled processes which are more rapid, efficient and hygienic than those employed on the traditional French farm. Rigorously selected at a time of collection, the milk is pasteurized before the cream is skimmed off by centrifuge. From this pasteurization, two dairy products are obtained: the concentrated milk fats (the cream) and skimmed milk. The intensity of the skimming determines the fat content of the resultant cream. The cream is finally pasteurized to ensure its keeping properties and then chilled. This stage is specific to commercial crème fraîche and the pressurized thermal treatment actually sterilizes the cream.

The cream gains its character from its satin-like texture and its taste. In order to achieve these special qualities, selected lactic cultures are added to the cream, which develops its distinctive aroma and light acidity, so highly appreciated by those who buy and eat it. This is what is referred to as the maturization of the cream. Crème fraîche is, therefore, a product that is truly 'alive'.

A GLOSSARY OF CRÈME FRAÎCHE
Many people are confused as to the differences between crème fraîche and British fresh dairy creams.

Fresh dairy cream, such as double and single cream, is obtained by creaming the fat that rises to the surface of cooled milk. The fat content of dairy creams varies according to type:

Single Cream is made from homogenized milk and contains a minimum of 18% fat.
Double Cream is not homogenized and contains a minimum of 48% fat.
Extra Thick Cream has the same fat content as double cream but is made from homogenized milk.
Clotted Cream, a West Country speciality, on the other hand, is made from milk which is first scalded and then skimmed and cooled quickly. It too contains a minimum of 48% fat.

However, none of these British dairy creams has the sharp taste and silky texture which are the hallmarks of crème fraîche.

Crème Fraîche
A traditional pasteurized, thick, cultured cream which has been 'matured' with the addition of lactic cultures. Its distinctive taste and characteristic velvety texture, make it an ideal ingredient to use in a wide variety of recipes. Standard crème fraîche has a fat content of 30%.

Crème Fraîche Light
A lighter crème fraîche which is a pasteurized, cultured blend of cream and skimmed milk, containing 15% fat – half that of standard crème fraîche.

Crème Fraîche Gastronomique
This is the richest of the crème fraîche varieties. It contains a third as much fat again as standard crème fraîche, giving it a consistency that is even more velvety – the perfect ingredient for those recipes that require that extra creamy richness.

NOTE: All crème fraîche products should be stored in a refrigerator.

Cream: Its Remarkable Nutritional Qualities

Milk, which is well-known for its important nutritional qualities, in turn gives birth to many other nutritious dairy foods, including cheese and butter. Cream is the product that is created midway through the cycle between milk and butter and it possesses many of the nutritional properties of both.

The cream that is lighter in fat than one would think!

It is a common assumption that crème fraîche is as rich in fat as butter. But that is not the case. Crème fraîche actually contains much more water and, therefore, contains far less fat than butter, margarine or olive oil. Its 30% fat content is two to three times lower than solid and semi-solid fats and oils.

The advantages of crème fraîche

Crème fraîche is a worthy descendant of milk. It combines tradition with modern taste and offers us numerous ways of using it creatively, in a wide variety of sweet and savoury recipes. A quick thumb through the tempting recipes in Cooking with Crème Fraîche will show just how versatile this special cream is, both in the kitchen and on the table!

Crème Fraîche . . .
The White Gold of Gastronomy

The pure whiteness and silkiness of crème fraîche seems to bring a sparkle to the eye of every gourmet, professional or amateur. It also appeals to all age groups; there are few French people, young or old, who have never dipped a finger into a bowl of Crème Chantilly before enjoying the accompanying dessert!

In France, crème fraîche is used extensively in soups, sauces, meat dishes, vegetables and desserts. The cream is generally added during the cooking of a dish – sometimes blended with egg yolks and sometimes used straight from the pot. Several spoonfuls of crème fraîche added to a basic hot soup, for example, transform it into something rather special.

Traditionally, salads are prepared with an oil and vinegar dressing. Some of them, in fact, can taste much better when complemented by a dressing based on crème fraîche and vinegar or lemon juice; this is definitely the case with cucumber, carrots and radishes.

It is, however, in desserts that crème fraîche really excels itself, adding a memorable finishing touch to a meal. However simple the dessert, whether it is a thin pancake filled with jam, or fresh strawberries, it is the 'touch of crème fraîche' that adds that crowning glory.

In fact, it is the essential spoonful or two of crème fraîche that gives the characteristic flavour and texture to so many traditional Norman recipes, especially the sweet ones.

Crème fraîche is one of the most versatile ingredients that a cook can have in the kitchen but there are certain guidelines to follow when using it. It is especially important to use the right variety of crème fraîche for a particular recipe in order to guarantee a successful result:

• Crème fraîche *must be added towards the end of cooking, perhaps just simmered for a minute or two (but not for longer, otherwise it tends to separate).*

• Crème fraîche gastronomique *is more robust and is perfectly suited to sauces. It lends a natural moistness and palatability to dishes that might otherwise be rather dry.*

- **Crème fraîche light** *is the ideal 'cooking cream' for those who appreciate flavour but wish to keep an eye on their weight. But take care – it is not as resilient as crème fraîche gastronomique and must only be added to a hot dish at the very last moment. It is a perfect accompaniment to fruits, vegetables and salads, as well as being a good low-calorie ingredient to use in recipes.*

For a perfect **Crème Chantilly,** *to top berry fruits and other desserts, use equal quantities of well-chilled crème fraîche and chilled milk. Beat over a bowl of ice, adding icing sugar to taste, until thick and light.*

To accompany savoury dishes, such as a warm vegetable tart or terrine, omit the icing sugar and add pepper to taste.

For a **Soured Cream,** *to serve as a cold sauce with vegetables, salads, starters or shellfish, beat crème fraîche light with a little lemon juice and seasoning to taste.*

Thanks to new techniques in its production and preservation, crème fraîche can always be in our refrigerators ready to use. Without crème fraîche, our cooking would lack imagination, flavour and texture.

NOTES ON WEIGHTS AND MEASURES
In all the recipes you will find two sets of weights and measurements: one metric and one Imperial. The gram/oz and kg/lb weights are standardized throughout.

All metric 'liquid' measurements are in millilitres (ml), apart from those for crème fraîche. This is because the Yoplait crème fraîche products are packed in centilitre (cl) tubs.

NOTE: *10 ml = 1 cl.*

GARLIC CREAM

Preparation: 20 minutes
Cooking: 20 minutes
Serves: 4

• 4 heads garlic
• 20 cl (6½ fl oz) Yoplait crème fraîche
• 100 ml (3½ fl oz) milk
• salt and pepper

• Peel the garlic cloves, split them and remove the green shoot. Place the garlic in a pan with just sufficient water to cover and bring to the boil. Drain the garlic cloves, cover with fresh water and bring to the boil once again. Repeat this process five more times, using fresh water on each occasion. The garlic should become quite soft and 'creamy'. Crush to a smooth paste using a fork or a pestle and mortar.
• Place the garlic in a heavy-based pan and gradually blend in the crème fraîche and milk. Season to taste. Bring to the boil gradually and simmer gently for 5 minutes. Taste the sauce and adjust seasoning if necessary.
• Serve hot with pasta, lamb, pork or lightly cooked green vegetables.

BASIL SAUCE

Preparation: 15 minutes
Cooking: 15 minutes
Serves: 4

• 2 bunches fresh basil
• 2 cloves garlic
• 10 g (⅓ oz) butter
• 30 cl (½ pint) Yoplait crème fraîche gastronomique
• salt and pepper

• Wash and dry the basil, separate the leaves and chop finely. Peel and crush the garlic.
• Melt the butter in a heavy-based pan. Add the basil and garlic and stir over a moderate heat for 1 minute. Stir in the crème fraîche and add seasoning to taste. Bring to the boil gradually and simmer gently for 10 minutes. Taste the sauce and adjust seasoning if necessary.
• Serve hot with fish, pasta or veal, or with steamed or boiled potatoes.

CURRY SAUCE

Preparation: 10 minutes
Cooking: 20 minutes
Serves: 4

• 1 large onion
• 30 g (1 oz) butter
• 1 tablespoon curry powder
• 1 tablespoon flour
• 600 ml (1 pint) chicken stock
• 20 cl (6½ fl oz) Yoplait crème fraîche gastronomique
• salt and pepper

• Peel and coarsely chop the onion.
• Melt the butter in a heavy-based pan, add the onion and cook gently for 2 to 3 minutes. Stir in the curry powder and flour and cook for 1 minute. Add the stock gradually, stirring continuously. Bring to the boil and simmer for 10 minutes. Blend in the crème fraîche, season to taste and simmer for 3 minutes. Taste the sauce and adjust seasoning if necessary.
• Serve hot with pork fillet or chops, cooked prawns, poached or hard-boiled eggs or grilled fish.

CRAYFISH SAUCE

Preparation: 5 minutes
Cooking: 20 minutes
Serves: 4

• 30 g (1 oz) butter
• 2 tablespoons flour
• 600 ml (1 pint) milk
• 40 cl (13 fl oz) Yoplait crème fraîche gastronomique
• 40 g (1½ oz) crayfish or lobster paste/cream*
• generous pinch cayenne pepper
• salt and pepper

• Melt the butter in a heavy-based pan. Stir in the flour and cook for 30 seconds. Add the milk gradually, stirring continuously and simmer for 10 minutes.
• Add the crème fraîche, shellfish paste, cayenne, and salt and pepper to taste. Stir well and simmer for a further 5 minutes.
• Serve with cooked shellfish, fish quenelles, fishcakes or pasta.

* Crayfish and lobster paste/cream is available in tubes and in small tins from good delicatessens and specialist food stores.

SAFFRON FISH SAUCE

Preparation: 30 minutes
Cooking: 30 minutes
Serves: 4

• 1 litre (2 pints) mussels
• 60 g (2 oz) butter
• 4 tablespoons flour
• 1 litre (1¾ pints) fish stock
• 2 pinches of saffron powder
• 40 cl (13 fl oz) Yoplait crème fraîche gastronomique
• pinch cayenne pepper
• salt and pepper

• Clean the mussels, discarding any with broken shells. Place the mussels in a large pan with 4 tablespoons of water. Cover the pan and cook the mussels over moderate heat for 15 minutes. Allow to cool. Then strain and reserve the cooking liquid, and shell the mussels.
• Melt the butter in a large heavy-based pan, stir in the flour and cook for 30 seconds. Stir in the fish stock and the strained mussel liquid gradually, and bring to the boil. Simmer for 10 minutes, stirring from time to time.
• Mix the saffron powder with 2 tablespoons of water and add to the sauce. Stir in the crème fraîche, add cayenne and salt and pepper to taste, and the shelled mussels. Simmer for a further 5 minutes. Taste the sauce and adjust seasoning if necessary.
• Serve hot with grilled, baked or poached fish, or with a warm fish mousse or terrine.

WHITE CHICKEN SAUCE

Preparation: 30 minutes
Cooking: 15 minutes
Serves: 4

• 1 litre (1¾ pints) white chicken stock
• 5 or 6 sprigs fresh chervil
• 60 g (2 oz) butter
• 4 tablespoons flour
• 20 cl (6½ fl oz) Yoplait crème fraîche gastronomique
• salt and pepper

• Place the stock and chervil in a pan and bring to the boil slowly. Remove from the heat and leave to infuse for 20 minutes. Remove the chervil.
• Melt the butter in a heavy-based pan, stir in the flour and cook for 30 seconds. Stir in the chicken stock gradually and bring to the boil. Simmer for 10 minutes, stirring from time to time. Blend in the crème fraîche and heat through. Season to taste.
• Serve hot with poached chicken, or with escalopes of turkey or veal.

Variation: Add some chopped or sliced button mushrooms, lightly cooked in butter, to the sauce.

MUSTARD SAUCE

Preparation: 15 minutes
Cooking: None
Serves: 4

- 6 tablespoons Dijon mustard
- salt and pepper
- juice of 1 lemon
- 30 cl (½ pint) Yoplait crème fraîche gastronomique, well chilled

- Mix the mustard, seasoning to taste and lemon juice together in a bowl. Gradually whisk in the crème fraîche, little by little, as if making mayonnaise.
- Serve with crudités, poached eggs, cold fish or salads.

APPLE SAUCE

Preparation: 20 minutes
Cooking: 20 minutes
Serves: 4

- 1 medium onion
- 3 Golden Delicious apples
- 1 orange
- 1 clove
- 3 pinches ground cinnamon
- salt and pepper
- 3 tablespoons white wine
- 3 tablespoons white wine vinegar
- 20 cl (6½ fl oz) Yoplait crème fraîche gastronomique

- Peel and finely chop the onion. Peel, halve and core the apples; chop the flesh. Thinly pare the rind from the orange and chop finely. Blanch the rind in boiling water for 1 minute and drain. Crush the clove and mix it with the cinnamon.
- Place the onion, apple, orange rind, spices and seasoning in a pan. Stir in the white wine and the vinegar. Cook over a gentle heat for 20 minutes, stirring from time to time. Press through a fine sieve.
- Place the apple purée in a clean pan. Stir in the crème fraîche and heat through over a gentle heat.
- Serve hot with goose, duck, roast pork or oily fish.

PRUNE SAUCE

Preparation: 15 minutes
Cooking: 20 minutes
Serves: 4

- 250 g (9 oz) pitted prunes
- 15 g (½ oz) butter
- 1 tablespoon flour
- finely grated rind and juice of 1 lemon
- 30 g (1 oz) caster sugar
- pinch ground cinnamon
- salt and pepper
- 20 cl (6½ fl oz) Yoplait crème fraîche gastronomique

- Place the prunes in a large pan and add sufficient water to cover. Bring to the boil and simmer steadily for 10 minutes. Drain the prunes, reserving their cooking liquid, and chop them finely.
- Melt the butter in a heavy-based pan. Stir in the flour and cook for 30 seconds. Stir in 300 ml (½ pint) of the prune liquid gradually, stirring continuously, and bring to the boil.
- Add the chopped prunes, lemon rind and juice, cinnamon, sugar, seasoning to taste and the crème fraîche. Simmer gently for 10 minutes, stirring from time to time. Taste the sauce and adjust seasoning if necessary.
- Serve with roast pork, roast veal or grilled escalopes or chops.

GAZPACHO

Preparation: 40 minutes
Chilling: 2 to 3 hours
Cooking: None
Serves: 6

- 8 slices white bread
- 3 cloves garlic
- 3 tablespoons olive oil
- 5 cumin seeds
- 2 tablespoons wine vinegar
- 6 tomatoes
- 1 green pepper
- 1 yellow pepper
- 1 large cucumber
- 20 black olives, pitted
- 2 medium onions
- 2 pinches dried marjoram
- 8 fresh mint leaves
- 2 pinches paprika
- 2 pinches cayenne pepper
- 500 ml (17 fl oz) tomato juice
- salt and pepper
- 20 cl (6½ fl oz) Yoplait crème fraîche gastronomique
- 4 tablespoons milk
- oil for frying croûtons

- Remove the crusts from four of the slices of bread and cut into small cubes. Peel the garlic cloves. Place the garlic and bread cubes in the bowl of a food processor with the olive oil, cumin seeds and vinegar; blend to a smooth paste.
- Blanch the tomatoes in boiling water for 1 minute; remove the skins and seeds and chop the tomato flesh finely (save the skins and seeds for use in a soup). Halve the peppers, remove the seeds and membrane and chop the flesh into small cubes. Peel the cucumber, remove the seeds and cut the flesh into small cubes. Finely chop the olives. Peel and finely chop the onions. Finely chop the marjoram and the mint.
- Place the bread 'paste' in a large bowl and add the chopped tomatoes, olives, half the peppers, the onions, cucumber, paprika, cayenne, herbs and salt and pepper to taste. Stir in the tomato juice and 250 ml (8½ fl oz) of very cold water. Mix well, then chill thoroughly.
- Cut the remaining bread into small cubes and fry in the hot oil until crisp and golden brown. Drain well on absorbent kitchen paper.
- Stir the crème fraîche and milk into the chilled soup. Ladle into soup bowls, adding an ice cube or two to each portion. Serve accompanied by the remaining chopped pepper and the croûtons.

Wine: Serve with a lightly chilled red wine: one with a good tannin content, such as Côte de Buzet or a notable Beaujolais Nouveau.

AUBERGINE AND COURGETTE RAMEKINS

Preparation: 20 minutes
Cooking: 55 minutes
Serves: 4

- 3 medium aubergines
- generous pinch ground cumin
- 2 egg yolks
- 10 cl (3½ fl oz) Yoplait crème fraîche
- salt and pepper
- 2 medium courgettes
- 10 g (⅓ oz) butter

- Preheat the oven to 220°C (425°F, Gas Mark 7).
- Wrap the aubergines in foil and bake in the oven for 30 minutes. Unwrap the aubergines, split them lengthways and scoop the flesh into a bowl with a teaspoon. Mix the aubergine flesh with the cumin, egg yolks, crème fraîche and seasoning to taste. Combine thoroughly and chill.
- Remove the stalk ends from the courgettes, wash them and cut lengthways into long slices. Blanch them for 3 minutes in boiling salted water. Drain them and gently pat dry on absorbent kitchen paper.
- Butter four ramekin dishes. Line the base and sides of each one with courgette slices, allowing the ends to overlap the rim. Fill with the aubergine purée and fold the ends of the courgette slices over the top. Stand the ramekins in a shallow ovenproof dish, adding sufficient hot water to come halfway up the sides of the dishes. Bake in the oven for 20 minutes. Leave to stand for 5 minutes before unmoulding on to serving plates. Serve cold, or while still warm if preferred, with a tomato sauce or well-flavoured herb vinaigrette.

Wine: Serve with a red Côtes de Provence or another well-rounded, fruity red.

SPRING SALAD

Preparation: 30 minutes
Cooking: 5 minutes
Serves: 4

• 200 g (7 oz) haricot verts (fine green beans)
• salt and pepper
• small bunch red radishes
• 2 medium new carrots
• 4 baby turnips
• heart of a batavia lettuce
• 2 shallots
• 3 tablespoons sherry vinegar or white wine vinegar
• 10 cl (3½ fl oz) Yoplait crème fraîche
• 100 ml (3½ fl oz) milk
• 4 pinches paprika
• 5 sprigs fresh chervil

• Top and tail the haricots verts. Cook them in boiling salted water for 5 minutes – they should still have a slight 'crunch'. Drain them and refresh in cold water. Drain once again.
• Clean the radishes, remove the leaves and feathery roots (save these for use in a soup). Cut the radishes into thin slices. Clean the carrots and cut lengthways into thin slices. Peel the turnips and grate them coarsely. Wash the batavia leaves and shake dry. Peel and finely chop the shallots.
• Place the vinegar in a bowl, add the crème fraîche, milk and shallots; mix well. Season to taste.
• Arrange the salad leaves and prepared vegetables on four serving plates, so as to give an attractive blend of colours. Spoon over the prepared dressing and garnish each salad with a few chervil leaves and a sprinkling of paprika.

Wine: A full-bodied white wine, such as a 'honeyed' Chardonnay, helps to cut through the vinegar in the dressing and bring out the natural sweetness in the vegetables.

ARTICHOKE AND PRAWN SALAD

Preparation: 30 minutes
Cooking: 25 minutes
Serves: 4

• 4 globe artichokes
• 1 lemon, cut in half
• 350 g (12 oz) shell-on prawns
• 1 small head radicchio
• 1 small feuille de chêne lettuce, or other lettuce of your choice
• 2 shallots
• 3 tablespoons sherry vinegar or white wine vinegar
• 5 cl (2 fl oz) Yoplait crème fraîche
• 50 ml (2 fl oz) milk
• salt and pepper
• 6 fresh chives, snipped

• Trim stalk ends of artichokes. Cut a thin slice from the pointed top of each artichoke and trim the tip of each leaf. Rub cut surfaces with the fleshy side of half a lemon. Cook the artichokes in a large pan of boiling water, to which you have added the other half lemon, for 25 minutes. Drain and cool under running water. Pull away the leaves from the artichokes and remove the hairy chokes, so as to expose the tender *fonds* or artichoke bottoms. (Keep the leaves for garnish, or for serving as dunks with a dip). Cut the *fonds* into thin slices.
• Remove the heads and shells from the prawns. Wash both varieties of salad and shake the leaves dry. Peel and finely chop the shallots.
• Place the vinegar in a bowl with the crème fraîche, milk and chopped shallots. Mix well and add seasoning to taste.
• Arrange the salad leaves decoratively on serving plates, add the prawns and artichoke slices and spoon over the prepared dressing. Sprinkle with snipped chives and garnish with a few pretty artichoke leaves, if liked.

Wine: A good Fino sherry is the best accompaniment to this salad, served well chilled.

BALTIC POTATO SALAD

Preparation: 30 minutes
Cooking: 15 minutes
Serves: 4

• 800 g (1¾ lb) medium, waxy potatoes
• 8 small rollmop herrings
• 2 medium, red-skinned onions
• 1 shallot
• 3 tablespoons white wine vinegar
• 10 cl (3½ fl oz) Yoplait crème fraîche
• 100 ml (3½ fl oz) milk
• salt and pepper
• sprigs of fresh dill

• Peel the potatoes and steam or boil them for 15 minutes. Cut them into slices, about 5 mm (¼ inch) thick, and allow to cool.
• Drain the rollmops thoroughly and cut into pieces. Peel and thinly slice the red onion. Peel and finely chop the shallot.
• Place the vinegar in a bowl with the crème fraîche, milk and shallot. Mix well and add seasoning to taste.
• Arrange the sliced potatoes on serving plates. Add the chopped rollmops and onion rings and spoon over the prepared dressing. Garnish with sprigs of dill.

Variation: Small pieces of smoked salmon or smoked eel can be used in place of rollmops, with a little lumpfish roe to garnish.

Wine: A well-chilled fruity white wine from the Loire region.

PASTA AND HAM SALAD

Preparation: 20 minutes
Cooking: about 8 minutes
Serves: 4

• 250 g (9 oz) pasta shapes, such as twistetti (spirals), farfalle (bows), lumache (snail shells) or creste di galli (cockscombs)
• ¼ cucumber
• 1 large ripe tomato
• 12 hazelnuts, shelled
• 1 shallot
• 2 slices cooked gammon (not too thin)
• 2 slices smoked ham (not too thin)
• 3 tablespoons sherry vinegar
• 10 cl (3½ fl oz) Yoplait crème fraîche light
• 1 Yoplait natural yogurt
• salt and pepper
• 12 small slices cured ham/meat, such as San Daniele, Coppa or viande des Grissons
• sprigs fresh chervil

• Cook the pasta in a large pan of boiling salted water for about 8 minutes, depending on pasta variety. Drain well and cool completely under cold running water. Drain once again.
• Cut the cucumber into thin slices. Halve the tomato, remove the seeds and dice the flesh. Chop the nuts. Peel and finely chop the shallot. Dice the gammon and smoked ham.
• Place the vinegar in a bowl with the crème fraîche, yogurt and shallot. Mix well and add seasoning to taste.
• Mix the cooled pasta with the chopped gammon and ham, cucumber, nuts and tomato, stir in the prepared dressing and mix well. Spoon on to serving plates, tucking a few curled slices of cured ham into each portion. Garnish with a few sprigs of chervil.

Wine: A young white Burgundy, a light white Chardonnay or a crisp rosé, all well chilled.

CHICKEN SALAD WITH CURRY DRESSING

Preparation: 30 minutes
Cooking: 3 minutes
Serves: 4

- 1 tablespoon creamed coconut
- 1 tablespoon curry powder
- 1 small batavia lettuce
- 2 medium chicory spears
- 1 Granny Smith apple
- juice of 1 lemon
- small bunch seedless grapes
- 2 cooked chicken breasts
- 2 tablespoons flaked almonds
- 10 cl (3½ fl oz) Yoplait crème fraîche light
- 1 Yoplait natural yogurt
- salt and pepper
- fresh flat-leaf parsley

- Place the creamed coconut and curry powder in a bowl with 3 tablespoons of hot water, mix well and leave to stand for 20 minutes.
- Separate the batavia and chicory leaves; wash and shake dry. Peel and core the apple, cut into slices and then into small dice. Place dice in a bowl with just sufficient water to cover and add the lemon juice. Separate the grapes from the bunch, wash and dry them. Thinly slice the chicken breasts.
- Lightly brown the almonds in a non-stick pan.
- Stir the crème fraîche and yogurt into the curry/coconut mixture. Add seasoning to taste.
- Arrange the batavia and chicory leaves on serving plates. Fan the chicken slices out on top of each salad and add the drained apple and grapes. Spoon the prepared dressing evenly over each salad. Sprinkle with browned almonds and garnish with parsley leaves.

Wine: A dry white Burgundy or a Soave.

CUCUMBER IN CREAM DRESSING

Preparation: 20 minutes
Chilling: 20 minutes
Cooking: None
Serves: 4

- 1 cucumber
- 1 clove garlic
- 1 shallot
- 3 tablespoons matured wine vinegar
- 10 cl (3½ fl oz) Yoplait crème fraîche
- 100 ml (3½ fl oz) milk
- salt and pepper
- 5 chives, snipped

- Peel the cucumber and cut into very thin slices. Plunge the cucumber slices into boiling water for just 30 seconds. Drain, cool under running water, drain once again and pat dry on absorbent kitchen paper.
- Peel and crush the garlic. Peel and finely chop the shallot.
- Put the vinegar in a bowl with the crème fraîche, milk, garlic and shallot. Mix well and add seasoning to taste. Stir in the cucumber slices so that they are evenly coated with the dressing. Chill, covered, for 20 minutes. Sprinkle with chives just before serving.

Variation: In summer, try adding a little chopped fresh mint.

Wine: A white Sancerre or a Pinot Grigio.

AVOCADO AND CRAB MOUSSE

Preparation: 30 minutes
Chilling: 4 hours
Cooking: None
Serves: 4

- 6 leaves gelatine
- 1 medium onion
- 200 g (7 oz) canned crabmeat
- 3 medium, ripe avocados
- juice of 1 lemon
- 10 cl (3½ fl oz) Yoplait crème fraîche
- 100 ml (3½ fl oz) milk
- 5 tablespoons canned seafood bisque

- Soak the leaves of gelatine in a little cold water to soften.
- Peel and finely chop the onion. Drain the crabmeat, removing any bones, and flake.
- Peel, halve and stone the avocados. Scoop the flesh into the bowl of a food processor, add the lemon juice and blend to a smooth purée.
- Beat the crème fraîche with the milk until smooth and creamy.
- Heat the bisque, add the squeezed leaves of soaked gelatine and stir until dissolved. Leave to cool.
- Place the avocado mixture in a bowl, add the onion, the bisque/gelatine mixture, crabmeat and the crème fraîche mixture. Mix lightly but thoroughly and add seasoning to taste.
- Dampen a savarin mould and add the prepared mixture, smoothing the surface. Chill for at least 4 hours. Unmould and serve with a green salad.

Wine: A 'flinty', well-chilled white wine, such as a crisp Sauvignon.

MUSSEL SALAD

Preparation: 35 minutes
Cooking: 15 minutes
Serves: 4

- 1 kg (2 lb) mussels
- 2 shallots
- 1 clove garlic
- 20 g (⅔ oz) butter
- 500 ml (17 fl oz) dry white wine
- salt and pepper
- 2 medium tomatoes
- 1 small batavia lettuce
- 5 chives
- 2 spring onions
- 5 tablespoons cider vinegar
- 20 cl (6½ fl oz) Yoplait crème fraîche light

- Wash and scrub the mussels, discarding any with broken shells. Peel and thinly slice the shallots. Peel and crush the garlic.
- Melt the butter in a large pan and add the shallots, garlic, mussels, white wine and seasoning. Bring to the boil and cook gently for 15 minutes, shaking the pan from time to time.
- Remove the cooked mussels from their shells; strain and reserve the cooking liquid.
- Halve the tomatoes and remove the centre seeds; cut the flesh into dice. Separate the batavia leaves; wash and shake dry. Chop the chives. Clean the onions and slice them thinly, including their top shoots.
- Place the vinegar in a bowl with the crème fraîche and 3 tablespoons of the mussel cooking liquid. Mix well and adjust seasoning to taste.
- Arrange the batavia leaves decoratively on serving plates with the mussels, diced tomatoes and onion slices. Spoon the prepared dressing evenly over each salad and sprinkle with chives.

Variation: The mussels can be added to the salad while still warm; add the shelled mussels, just before serving, and use a few cooked mussels still in their shells as garnish.

Wine: A lively and fruity, well-chilled Muscadet.

KIPPER MOUSSE

Preparation: 20 minutes
Chilling: 2 to 3 hours
Cooking: None
Serves: 5 to 6

- 4 small kippers, filleted
- 1 small red onion
- 3 to 4 sprigs fresh dill
- 15 cl (5 fl oz) Yoplait crème fraîche
- 150 ml (5 fl oz) milk
- pepper

- Remove all visible bones from the kipper fillets. Cut the fillets into pieces and place in the bowl of a food processor; blend to a fairly smooth purée.
- Peel and finely chop the onion. Chop the dill. Mix the onion and dill into the kipper purée.
- Beat the crème fraîche and milk until smooth and creamy; mix into the kipper purée. Season to taste with pepper. Spoon the mousse into a terrine dish. Cover, and chill in the freezer for 2 to 3 hours.
- Serve very cold with fingers of hot toast.

Variation: This makes a delicious, easy topping for canapés.

Wine: The slight 'smokiness' of a Pouilly Fumé is a perfect match to the characteristic flavour of the fish mousse.

SMOKED COD'S ROE PATE

Preparation: 20 minutes
Chilling: 2 hours
Cooking: None
Serves: 4

- 100 g (3½ oz) stale white bread
- 175 g (6 oz) smoked cod's roe
- 5 cl (2 fl oz) Yoplait crème fraîche light
- 50 ml (2 fl oz) milk
- juice of ½ lemon
- 2 pinches paprika
- pepper

- Crumble or coarsely grate the bread. Split the skin of the cod's roe; scoop the roe into the bowl of a food processor. Add the bread, crème fraîche and milk, and blend to a fairly smooth paste. Add the lemon juice, paprika and pepper to taste.
- Place in the mixture in a small terrine and smooth the surface. Cover and chill for 2 hours.
- Serve with fingers of hot toast, or with warm blinis, wedges of lemon and a bowl of chilled Yoplait crème fraîche.

Wine: A fresh-flavoured Sancerre.

MUSSEL AND COCKLE SOUP

Preparation: 30 minutes
Cooking: 30 minutes
Serves: 4

• 500 g (1 lb) mussels
• 2 shallots
• 2 cloves garlic
• 5 sprigs fresh flat-leaf parsley
• 3 tomatoes
• 30 g (1 oz) butter
• 200 ml (6½ fl oz) dry white wine
• pinch cayenne pepper
• salt and pepper
• 300 ml (½ pint) shelled cockles (not in vinegar)
• 1 egg yolk
• 20 cl (6½ fl oz) Yoplait crème fraîche light

• Wash and scrub the mussels, discarding any with broken shells. Peel and thinly slice the shallots. Peel and crush the garlic. Roughly chop the parsley.
• Blanch the tomatoes in boiling water for 1 minute, remove the skins and the centre seeds and cut the flesh into dice.
• Melt the butter in a large pan, add the shallots and cook over a moderate heat for 3 minutes. Add the mussels, tomatoes, garlic, white wine, cayenne, salt and pepper, and 1 litre (1¾ pints) of water. Cover and cook over a moderate heat for 20 minutes.
• Remove the mussels with a slotted spoon; keep on one side.
• Boil the cooking liquid rapidly for 3 minutes. Transfer to a food processor and blend until smooth. Add the mussels and cockles and stir in the blended egg yolk and crème fraîche. Heat through gently and adjust seasoning to taste.
• Serve piping hot, with fried garlic croûtons or warm crusty bread.

Wine: A fairly fruity white wine, such as Entre-Deux-Mers, or a deep golden Chardonnay.

SMOOTH MUSHROOM SOUP

Preparation: 20 minutes
Cooking: 35 minutes
Serves: 4

• 400 g (14 oz) button mushrooms
• 3 shallots
• 1 clove garlic
• 4 sprigs fresh chervil
• 40 g (1½ oz) butter
• 1 teaspoon curry powder
• salt and pepper
• 10 cl (3½ fl oz) Yoplait crème fraîche light
• 1 teaspoon cornflour

• Wash, dry and thinly slice the mushrooms. Peel and chop the shallots and the garlic. Snip the chervil into leaves.
• Melt the butter in a large pan, add the shallots and garlic and cook over a moderate heat for 2 minutes. Add the mushrooms and cook for a further 5 minutes. Sprinkle with the curry powder and chervil. Add 1.5 litres (2½ pints) of water and seasoning to taste. Cover, bring to the boil and simmer gently for 20 minutes.
• Blend the soup in a food processor until smooth. Pour in a clean pan and add the crème fraîche, then add the cornflour blended with a little water. Bring to the boil and stir over a gentle heat for 5 minutes until the soup is thick and smooth. Adjust seasoning to taste.

Wine: A full white Burgundy or an amber Chardonnay.

ASPARAGUS PASTRIES

Preparation: 30 minutes
Cooking: 20 minutes
Serves: 4

- 250 g (9 oz) puff pastry
- 1 egg yolk
- 700 g (1¾ lb) green asparagus
- 1 large tomato
- 5 fresh chives
- 1 shallot
- 20 g (⅔ oz) butter
- 100 ml (3½ fl oz) dry white wine
- 20 cl (6½ fl oz) Yoplait crème fraîche
- salt and pepper

- Preheat the oven to 220°C (425°F, Gas Mark 7).
- Roll out the pastry to a thickness of 1 cm (½ inch). Cut four rectangles, each about 15 × 8 cm (6 × 3¼ inches). Beat the egg yolk with 1 tablespoon of water and glaze the top of each pastry rectangle. Using a sharp knife, mark the top of each one in diamond shapes. Place on a non-stick baking sheet and bake for 20 minutes.
- Meanwhile, trim and clean the asparagus; steam for 15 minutes. Halve the tomato, remove the seeds and cut the flesh into dice. Chop the chives. Peel and slice the shallot.
- Melt the butter in a pan, add the shallot and cook quickly for 1 minute. Add the wine and simmer until reduced by half. Stir in the crème fraîche, add seasoning to taste and bring to the boil; simmer for 5 minutes.
- Cut each hot pastry rectangle in half horizontally. Place the base pastry layers on warm serving plates. Top with a layer of cooked asparagus, a sprinkling of tomato and a little sauce; sandwich with the top pastry layers. Spoon a little extra sauce around each one and sprinkle with chives. Serve immediately.

Wine: A dry, but aromatic white wine, such as a Graves.

SPINACH SOUFFLE

Preparation: 20 minutes
Cooking: 35 minutes
Serves: 4

- 1 kg (2 lb) spinach
- 80 g (2¾ oz) butter
- 4 eggs
- salt and pepper
- 80 g (2¾ oz) flour
- 400 ml (13 fl oz) milk
- 10 cl (3½ fl oz) Yoplait crème fraîche
- generous pinch freshly ground nutmeg
- 50 g (1¾ oz) Gruyère cheese, grated

- Preheat the oven to 220°C (425°F, Gas Mark 7). Grease the inside of a soufflé dish and sprinkle very lightly with flour.
- Remove stalks from the spinach leaves; wash, shake dry and tear into pieces. Melt 20 g (¾ oz) of the butter in a large pan, add the spinach and cook for 10 minutes over a moderate heat. Drain off any excess liquid and allow the spinach to cool.
- Separate the egg yolks from the whites; keep the whites on one side. Stir the yolks into the spinach and season to taste.
- Melt the remaining butter in a large, heavy-based saucepan, stir in the flour, and cook over a gentle heat for 30 seconds. Add the milk gradually, stirring continuously. Cook the sauce gently for 5 minutes. Mix the sauce with the cooled spinach, crème fraîche, nutmeg and grated cheese. Adjust seasoning to taste.
- Whisk the egg whites until stiff but not dry and fold lightly but thoroughly into the spinach sauce. Transfer the mixture to the prepared soufflé dish. Draw the rounded blade of a small knife between the mixture and the sides of the dish – this helps the soufflé to rise evenly. Bake for 20 minutes, until well risen and golden. Serve immediately.

Wine: A crisp white wine, with a slightly 'grassy' flavour, such as Frascati.

GREEN OLIVE TART

Preparation: 30 minutes
Cooking: 40 minutes
Serves: 4

Pastry:
• 225 g (8 oz) flour
• pinch salt
• 125 g (4½ oz) butter

Filling:
• 250 g (9 oz) pitted green olives
• 30 cl (½ pint) Yoplait crème fraîche
• 2 egg yolks
• salt and pepper

• Preheat the oven to 220°C (425°F, Gas Mark 7).
For the pastry:
• Sieve the flour and salt into a bowl, add the butter in small pieces and rub in finely with the fingertips. Add sufficient cold water to mix to a smooth but firm dough. Wrap and keep cool.
For the filling:
• Chop the olives coarsely. Place the crème fraîche in a bowl with the egg yolks and seasoning to taste; mix well. Add the chopped olives.
• Roll out the pastry and use to line a 23 cm (9 inch) fluted flan tin; press up the edges well. Pour in the prepared filling and bake for 40 minutes.
• Serve hot or cold, either as a starter or cut into small pieces with aperitifs.

Wine: A hearty red from the southern part of France – a Bandol or a Côtes de Provence.

PEPPER AND COURGETTE TART

Preparation: 40 minutes
Cooking: 45 minutes
Serves: 6

Pastry:
• 225 g (8 oz) flour
• pinch salt
• 125 g (4½ oz) butter

Filling:
• 4 tomatoes
• 1 small red pepper
• 1 small green pepper
• 1 small yellow pepper
• 2 medium courgettes
• 2 medium onion
• 2 cloves garlic
• 6 black olives, pitted
• 40 g (1½ oz) butter
• pinch dried savory
• salt and pepper
• 30 cl (½ pint) Yoplait crème fraîche
• 3 egg yolks
• 5 or 6 basil leaves

• Preheat the oven to 220°C (425°F, Gas Mark 7).
For the pastry:
• Sieve the flour and salt into a bowl, add the butter in small pieces and rub in finely with the fingertips. Add sufficient cold water to mix to a smooth but firm dough. Wrap and keep cool.
For the filling:
• Roughly chop the tomatoes. Halve and de-seed the peppers; cut into thin slices. Slice the courgettes. Peel and slice the onions and the garlic. Roughly chop the olives.
• Roll out the pastry and use to line a 23 cm (9 inch) loose-bottomed, fluted flan tin; press up the edges. Prick the base of the pastry, line with paper and beans, and bake 'blind' for 15 minutes.
• Meanwhile, melt the butter in a large pan and cook the onions gently for 3 minutes. Add the peppers, courgettes, olives, garlic, savory and seasoning to taste. Cook over a moderate heat for 10 minutes, stirring from time to time. Add the tomatoes.
• Place the crème fraîche in a bowl with the egg yolks and seasoning to taste. Mix well and add the drained cooked vegetables. Remove the paper and beans and fill the pastry case with the filling. Return to the oven for a further 30 minutes.
• Serve hot or cold, garnished with basil leaves and accompanied by a mixed salad.

Wine: A similar red wine to those suggested for the Green Olive Tart (above).

LORRAINE TART

Preparation: 45 minutes
Chilling: 24 hours
Cooking: 50 minutes
Serves: 6

• 400 g (14 oz) boned rabbit
• 400 g (14 oz) boned tender veal
• 3 shallots
• 150 ml (5 fl oz) dry white wine
• 3 tablespoons brandy
• 1 clove
• 2 juniper berries
• 1 bay leaf
• 3 large sprigs fresh parsley
• 400 g (14 oz) puff pastry
• 4 egg yolks
• 20 cl (6½ fl oz) Yoplait crème fraîche
• 200 ml (6½ fl oz) milk
• salt and pepper

• Cut the rabbit and veal into pieces about 2 × 2 cm (¾ × ¾ inch). Peel and slice the shallots.
• Mix the wine, brandy and spices in a shallow dish, add the parsley, torn into pieces, shallots and meat pieces. Stir to coat the meat in the marinade. Cover and chill for 24 hours.
• Drain the pieces of meat, discarding the spices. Strain the marinade, reserving both the juices and the shallots.
• Preheat the oven to 220°C (425°F, Gas Mark 7).
• Divide the pastry into one-third and two-thirds. Roll out the larger piece and use to line a loose-bottomed torten tin, about 20 cm (8 inches) in diameter – leave any pastry that overlaps the sides. Dampen the pastry rim and fill with the meat and shallots. Roll out the smaller piece of pastry and use to cover the meat filling. Trim off excess pastry and pinch the two layers of pastry together neatly.
• Beat one of the egg yolks with 2 tablespoons of water and brush the glaze evenly over the top of the pastry. Make a hole in the centre of the pastry lid and fix with a small 'chimney' of rolled baking parchment.
• Place the crème fraîche in a bowl with the remaining egg yolks, 5 tablespoons of the marinade and seasoning to taste; mix well. Carefully pour this mixture through the paper chimney.
• Bake for 30 minutes. Reduce the temperature to 190°C (375°F, Gas Mark 5) and bake for a further 20 minutes.
• Serve straight from the oven with a salad.

Wine: A light, red Burgundy or a really fruity rosé.

FROGS' LEGS WITH PARSLEY

Preparation: 15 minutes
Cooking: 20 minutes
Serves: 4

• 4 'skewers' of frogs' legs
• 4 shallots
• 4 cloves garlic
• 4 large sprigs fresh parsley
• 100 g (3½ oz) butter
• 100 ml (3½ fl oz) dry white wine
• 15 cl (5 fl oz) Yoplait crème fraîche light
• salt and pepper

• Remove the frogs' legs from the skewers; rinse and dry them. Peel and slice the shallots and garlic. Chop the parsley.
• Melt half the butter in a large frying pan without allowing it to colour. Add the frogs' legs and cook gently for 10 minutes, turning them from time to time. Keep warm.
• Melt the remaining butter in a pan; add the shallots and cook over a moderate heat for 5 minutes. Add the wine and garlic, and allow to bubble gently until reduced by half. Gradually whisk in the crème fraîche and add seasoning to taste. Simmer for 3 minutes.
• Spoon the cooked frogs' legs on to warm serving plates, spoon over the sauce and sprinkle with chopped parsley.

Wine: One of the light and refreshing Eastern European Chardonnays.

* Frogs' legs can be bought fresh from many speciality butchers in the UK. Alternatively, it is possible to buy them frozen from quality food stores.

SCRAMBLED EGGS WITH HADDOCK

Preparation: 20 minutes
Chilling: 2 hours
Cooking: 15 minutes
Serves: 4

• 300 g (10 oz) haddock fillet
• 600 ml (1 pint) milk
• 8 eggs
• salt and pepper
• 80 g (2¾ oz) butter
• 4 tablespoons Yoplait crème fraîche gastronomique
• sprigs fresh dill

• Place the haddock in a shallow dish and pour over half the milk. Cover and chill for 2 hours. Drain the fish, discarding the milk.
• Place the fish in a shallow pan with the remaining milk. Bring to the boil and simmer gently for 10 minutes. Drain the cooked haddock and flake the flesh, removing any stray bones.
• Crack the eggs into a bowl and beat lightly, adding seasoning to taste.
• Melt 50 g (1¾ oz) of the butter in a heavy-based pan, add the beaten eggs and the flaked fish, and cook very gently and slowly, stirring the egg until it forms soft, creamy flakes. Remove from the heat and stir in the remaining butter in small pieces and the crème fraîche – there will be enough heat in the pan to warm it through.
• Serve on small slices of bread fried in butter, or on toast, garnished with sprigs of dill.

Wine: A light rosé or, for a quite different flavour partnership, a well-chilled Fino sherry.

BAKED EGGS WITH AVOCADO

Preparation: 15 minutes
Cooking: 5 minutes
Serves: 4

• 1 shallot
• 1 ripe avocado
• juice of ½ lemon
• salt and pepper
• 30 g (1 oz) butter
• 15 cl (5 fl oz) Yoplait crème fraîche
• 4 fresh chives, snipped

• Preheat the oven to 190°C (375°F, Gas Mark 5).
• Peel the shallot. Peel, halve and stone the avocado. Scoop the avocado flesh into the bowl of a food processor and add the lemon juice, shallot and seasoning to taste. Blend to a fine purée.
• Butter four ramekin dishes. Spoon a little crème fraîche and then a quarter of the avocado purée into each one. Season to taste and carefully crack an egg into each ramekin. Top with a little more crème fraîche and season once again.
• Stand the ramekins in a roasting tin and add sufficient hot water to come halfway up the sides of the ramekins. Bake for 5 minutes, until just set.
• Serve piping hot, sprinkled with snipped chives and accompanied by fingers of toast.

Wine: A soft Beaujolais or perhaps a lightish red Rioja.

BAKED SCALLOPS IN SAFFRON SAUCE

Preparation: 40 minutes
Cooking: 25 minutes
Serves: 4

- 24 scallops, with top and bottom shells
- 3 shallots
- 20 g (⅔ oz) butter
- 100 ml (3½ fl oz) dry white wine
- 10 cl (3½ fl oz) Yoplait crème fraîche
- pinch saffron strands
- 200 g (7 oz) flour
- 1 egg yolk
- rock salt

- Preheat the oven to 200°C (400°F, Gas Mark 6).
- Clean the scallops carefully. Select four pairs of perfect shells; wash and dry them. Peel and slice the shallots.
- Melt the butter in a pan. Add the shallots and cook gently for 3 minutes. Add the white wine and cook until reduced by half. Add the crème fraîche, saffron and seasoning and bring to the boil. Remove the sauce from the heat.
- Place the flour in a bowl and mix with sufficient water to make a firm, pliable dough. Roll out and cut four strips, each 25 × 3 cm (10 × 1¼ inches).
- Sit the four curved shells on a baking sheet, surrounding each one with a small bed of rock salt so that it stands upright. Place 3 scallops in each shell and spoon over a little saffron sauce. Cover with the four reserved flat shells. Carefully fix a strip of dough around the join on each pair of shells, pinching it to seal. Beat the egg yolk with 2 tablespoons of water and glaze the dough strips. Bake for 15 minutes.
- As the pastry strip is broken on each portion, the most wonderful scallop aroma is released from the shells!

Wine: A well-chilled Sancerre or Pouilly Fumé.

CRAB BRIOCHES

Preparation: 30 minutes
Cooking: 18 minutes
Serves: 4

- 4 small brioches
- 200 g (7 oz) canned crabmeat
- 2 spring onions
- 20 g (⅔ oz) butter
- 20 cl (6½ fl oz) Yoplait crème fraîche
- 1 egg yolk
- pinch cayenne pepper
- 2 pinches paprika
- salt and pepper

- Preheat the oven to 180°C (350°F, Gas Mark 4).
- Remove the 'hat' from each brioche. Carefully hollow out most of the centre crumb; reserve half of this. Drain the crabmeat, removing any bones, and flake it.
- Slice the spring onions, including the green ends. Melt the butter in a small pan and cook the spring onions gently for 2 minutes.
- Place the crème fraîche in a bowl with the egg yolk, crabmeat, reserved brioche crumb, spring onions, cayenne, paprika and seasoning to taste; mix well. Fill the hollowed brioches with the crabmeat mixture and replace the 'hats'.
- Cook the brioches in the oven for 15 minutes. Serve warm with some mixed salad leaves.

Wine: A light white Burgundy or the Italian freshness of Pinot Grigio.

SPICED MUSSELS

Preparation: 30 minutes
Cooking: 25 minutes
Serves: 4

- 1 kg (2 lb) mussels
- 2 shallots
- 1 clove garlic
- 20 g (⅔ oz) butter
- 2 chillis
- 1 star anise
- 2 cardamom seeds
- 1 clove
- 6 sprigs fresh coriander
- 1 tablespoon coriander seeds
- 200 ml (6½ fl oz) dry white wine
- salt and pepper
- 20 cl (6½ fl oz) Yoplait crème fraîche light

- Wash and scrub the mussels, discarding any with broken shells. Peel and slice the shallots and the garlic.
- Melt the butter in a large pan, add the shallots and cook gently for 2 minutes. Add the mussels, garlic, chillis, star anise, cardamom, clove, coriander sprigs, coriander seeds, wine and seasoning to taste. Cover and cook over a moderate heat for 15 minutes, stirring the mussels from time to time. Stir in the crème fraîche and cook gently for a further 5 minutes.
- Serve immediately with hot crusty bread.

Wine: A white wine of character which can match the distinct spiciness of this dish; for example, a Graves, with a citrus, fruity base.

NOODLES WITH SMOKED SALMON

Preparation: 10 minutes
Cooking: 10 minutes
Serves: 4

- 4 slices smoked salmon
- 1 shallot
- 20 g (⅔ oz) butter
- 20 cl (6½ fl oz) Yoplait crème fraîche light
- salt and pepper
- 300 g (10 oz) fresh tagliatelle
- juice of ½ lemon
- 1 egg yolk
- 50 g (1¾ oz) orange lumpfish roe
- sprigs fresh dill

- Cut the smoked salmon into strips and then into small dice. Peel and finely chop the shallot.
- Melt the butter in a pan; add the chopped shallot and cook gently for 2 minutes. Add the crème fraîche, smoked salmon and seasoning to taste. Bring to the boil, remove from the heat and keep on one side.
- Cook the tagliatelle in boiling water until just tender – about 3 to 4 minutes. Drain well.
- Stir the lemon juice and egg yolk into the sauce. Place the drained pasta in a clean pan and add the sauce. Heat through gently for 1 to 2 minutes.
- Spoon on to warmed serving plates and garnish with lumpfish roe and sprigs of dill.

Variation: This recipe can also be prepared using strips of bacon or smoked duck in place of the salmon.

Wine: A delicate, nutty white wine, such as a Chablis.

SMOKED SALMON PANCAKES

Preparation: 30 minutes
Cooking: 30 minutes
Serves: 6

Pancake batter:
- 125 g (4½ oz) flour
- pinch salt
- 3 eggs
- 30 g (1 oz) butter, melted
- 500 ml (17 fl oz) milk
- extra butter for cooking pancakes

Filling:
- 6 slices smoked salmon, cut into small pieces
- 25 cl (8 fl oz) Yoplait crème fraîche gastronomique
- several small sprigs fresh dill
- salt and pepper

• Preheat the oven to 180°C (350°F, Gas Mark 4).
For the batter:
• Place the flour, salt, eggs and melted butter in a bowl; beat until smooth. Gradually beat in the milk.
• Using a lightly buttered pancake pan, cook twelve thin pancakes. Keep them warm.
For the filling:
• Place a little smoked salmon on each pancake. Add a little crème fraîche, a few sprigs of dill and seasoning to taste. Roll up the pancakes and place them in a shallow ovenproof dish. Spoon over the remaining crème fraîche and sprinkle with extra dill.
• Heat through in the oven for 15 minutes. Serve piping hot.

Wine: A well-chilled Sancerre is perfect with the pancakes.

WARM SALMON MOULD

Preparation: 30 minutes
Cooking: 40 minutes
Serves: 4

- 400 g (14 oz) fresh salmon
- 1 shallot
- 1 thick slice smoked salmon
- several leaves young spinach
- 20 cl (6½ fl oz) Yoplait crème fraîche
- 3 egg yolks
- 100 ml (3½ fl oz) milk
- pinch cayenne pepper
- salt and pepper
- 10 g (⅓ oz) butter

• Preheat the oven to 180°C (350°F, Gas Mark 4).
• Steam the salmon for 10 minutes. Remove the skin and bones. Peel the shallot.
• Place the salmon, smoked salmon and shallot in the bowl of a food processor; blend until well mixed.
• Wash the spinach leaves and blanch them in boiling water for 30 seconds. Drain them and dry them carefully.
• Place the crème fraîche in a bowl with the egg yolks, milk, salmon mixture, cayenne and seasoning to taste; mix well.
• Grease a large, shallow mould (metal or ovenproof china) with the butter. Fill with half the prepared salmon mixture, lay the spinach leaves on top and then add the remaining salmon mixture.
• Stand the mould in a roasting tin and add sufficient hot water to come half way up the sides of the mould. Cook in the oven for 40 minutes. Unmould and serve hot with a salad.

Wine: A well-chilled, fruity Muscadet or a Frascati.

COURGETTE AND HERB TERRINE

Preparation: 45 minutes
Cooking: 2 hours
Chilling: 4 hours
Serves: 6

• 300 g (10 oz) onions
• 2 kg (4¼ lb) courgettes
• 4 slices bread
• 50 ml (2 fl oz) milk
• 50 g (1¾ oz) fresh tarragon
• 50 g (1¾ oz) fresh mint
• 60 g (2 oz) butter
• 6 eggs
• 20 cl (6½ fl oz) Yoplait crème fraîche
• 2 pinches ground nutmeg
• salt and pepper
• 400 g (14 oz) sorrel or young spinach

• Peel and thinly slice the onions. Top and tail the courgettes and cut into thin slices. Soak the bread in the milk. Chop the tarragon and mint.
• Melt two-thirds of the butter in a pan, add the onions and fry for 4 minutes. Add the courgettes and cook gently for a further 20 minutes, stirring from time to time. Drain the vegetables.
• Preheat the oven to 160°C (325°F, Gas Mark 3).
• Beat the eggs with the crème fraîche, chopped tarragon and mint, nutmeg, seasoning to taste, courgettes and onions, and the squeezed bread.
• Wash and dry the sorrel. Cook in the remaining butter for just 30 seconds.
• Grease a terrine and spread half the vegetable mixture in a layer in the bottom. Top with the lightly cooked sorrel and then the remaining vegetable mixture. Cover with a piece of greased foil or parchment. Stand in a roasting dish and add sufficient hot water to come halfway up the sides of the terrine. Cook for 1½ hours.
• Leave to cool and then chill for 4 hours.
• Serve with crème fraîche mixed with chopped fresh herbs.

Wine: A young Beaujolais.

MUSHROOM TERRINE

Preparation: 35 minutes
Cooking: 1 hour
Chilling: 4 hours
Serves: 6

• 2 kg (4¼ lb) mushrooms, preferably pleurotes or chanterelles
• 4 shallots
• 2 cloves garlic
• 50 g (1¾ oz) butter
• 100 ml (3½ fl oz) dry white wine
• salt and pepper
• 3 eggs
• 25 cl (8 fl oz) Yoplait crème fraîche
• 6 sprigs fresh chervil

• Preheat the oven to 180°C (350°F, Gas Mark 4).
• Clean the mushrooms. Peel and slice the shallots and the garlic.
• Melt the butter in a pan, fry the shallots for 2 minutes. Add the wine and reduce by a half. Add the mushrooms, garlic and seasoning to taste. Cook for 10 minutes, stirring occasionally.
• Beat the eggs with the crème fraîche and seasoning to taste. Add the drained mushrooms and the leaves of the chervil and mix well.
• Grease a terrine and add the mushroom mixture. Cover with a piece of greased foil or parchment. Stand in a roasting tin and add sufficient hot water to come halfway up the sides of the terrine. Cook for 45 minutes.
• Leave to cool and then chill for 4 hours.
• Unmould and serve with a fresh tomato sauce.

Wine: A fresh, 'clean' and stylish white wine, such as Vouvray.

LEEK TERRINE

Preparation: 30 minutes
Cooking: 1 hour
Chilling: 4 hours
Serves: 6

• 3 kg (6½ lb) leeks
• 2 shallots
• 50 g (1¾ oz) butter
• 3 eggs
• 25 cl (8 fl oz) Yoplait crème fraîche gastronomique
• 2 pinches cayenne pepper
• salt and pepper

• Preheat the oven to 180°C (350°F, Gas Mark 4).
• Clean the leeks and slice them finely. Peel and chop the shallots.
• Melt the butter in a pan, add the shallots and leeks and fry gently for 15 minutes, stirring from time to time.
• Beat the eggs with the crème fraîche, cayenne and seasoning to taste. Add the drained shallots and leeks and mix well.
• Grease a terrine and add the leek mixture. Cover with a piece of greased foil or baking parchment. Stand in a roasting tin and add sufficient hot water to come halfway up the sides of the terrine. Cook for 45 minutes.
• Leave to cool and then chill for 4 hours.
• Serve with hot toast or with slices of smoked salmon.

Wine: A well-chilled Muscadet.

SALMON AND SPINACH TERRINE

Preparation: 30 minutes
Cooking: 40 minutes
Chilling: 4 hours
Serves: 6

• 2 shallots
• 1 kg (2 lb) fresh salmon
• 2 egg yolks
• 25 cl (8 fl oz) Yoplait crème fraîche
• 2 sprigs fresh chervil
• 400 g (14 oz) spinach leaves
• 20 g (⅔ oz) butter

• Preheat the oven to 180°C (350°F, Gas Mark 4).
• Peel the shallots. Remove all skin and bones from the salmon. Cut the flesh into fine escalopes, keeping four good-sized ones on one side. Place the rest of the salmon in the bowl of a food processor with the shallots and seasoning to taste; blend coarsely.
• Beat the egg yolks with the crème fraîche and seasoning, to taste. Add the blended salmon and the leaves of chervil.
• Wash and dry the spinach, removing any tough stalks. Blanch the spinach in boiling water for 10 seconds; drain and dry.
• Generously butter a terrine and line the base and sides with some of the spinach leaves. Spoon one-third of the salmon mixture into the terrine and top with two of the reserved salmon escalopes. Add a further one-third of the salmon mixture and the remaining two escalopes. Finally add the remaining salmon mixture and cover with the remaining spinach. Cover with a piece of greased foil or parchment. Stand in a roasting tin and add sufficient hot water to come halfway up the sides of the terrine. Cook for 40 minutes.
• Leave to cool and then chill for 4 hours. Serve with a salad garnish.

Wine: A nutty Alsace Riesling.

COD AND CRAYFISH TERRINE

Preparation: 40 minutes
Cooking: 1 hour
Chilling: 4 hours
Serves: 6

- 12 langoustines (crayfish)
- 3 shallots
- 1 clove garlic
- 500 g (1 lb) button mushrooms
- 40 g (1½ oz) butter
- 600 g (1¼ lb) cod fillet
- 25 cl (8 fl oz) Yoplait crème fraîche
- 3 egg yolks
- salt and pepper

- Head, shell and tail the langoustines. Peel and chop the shallots and garlic. Clean the mushrooms and chop them roughly.
- Preheat the oven to 180°C (350°F, Gas Mark 4).
- Melt the butter and fry the shallots, garlic and mushrooms for 10 minutes, stirring from time to time.
- Cut the cod into cubes, place in the bowl of a food processor and blend fairly coarsely.
- Beat the crème fraîche with the egg yolks and the seasoning to taste; mix with the blended cod.
- Butter a terrine and add one-third of the cod mixture, six crayfish and half the mushrooms. Add a layer of cod, six more crayfish and the remaining mushrooms. Finally add the remaining cod mixture. Cover with a piece of greased foil or parchment. Stand in a roasting tin and add sufficient hot water to come halfway up the sides of the terrine. Cook for 45 minutes.
- Leave to cool and then chill for 4 hours. Unmould and serve with a salad garnish.

Wine: For a change, the fresh fruitiness of a Corsican white.

CHICKEN AND PRAWN TERRINE

Preparation: 40 minutes
Cooking: 1 hour
Chilling: 4 hours
Serves: 6

- 1 medium chicken
- 4 shallots
- ½ medium head fennel
- 1.5 kg (3¼ lb) prawns in shells
- 50 g (1¾ oz) butter
- 200 ml (6½ fl oz) dry white wine
- 3 egg yolks
- 20 cl (6½ fl oz) Yoplait crème fraîche gastronomique
- salt and pepper

- Remove the two chicken breasts neatly. Cut all the remaining chicken flesh from the carcass in pieces. Peel and slice the shallots. Finely slice the fennel. Head, shell and tail the prawns.
- Melt 40 g (1½ oz) of the butter in a pan and fry the shallots and fennel for 2 to 3 minutes. Add the wine and reduce by a half. Add the prawns and cook for 2 minutes. Season to taste.
- Preheat the oven to 180°C (350°F, Gas Mark 4).
- Place the chicken flesh, apart from the breasts, in the bowl of a food processor. Blend until fairly smooth. Cut the breasts into slices.
- Beat the egg yolks with the crème fraîche and prawns; add the chicken mixture and mix well.
- Grease a terrine with the remaining butter. Spoon one-third of the chicken and prawn mixture into the terrine and top with half the chicken slices. Add another third of the chicken and prawn mixture and the remaining chicken slices. Finally add the remaining chicken and prawn mixture. Cover with a piece of greased foil or parchment. Stand in a roasting tin and add sufficient hot water to come halfway up the sides of the terrine. Cook for 50 minutes.
- Leave to cool and then chill for 4 hours. Serve with hot toast.

Wine: A slightly spicy Provençal white.

CHICKEN TERRINE WITH GREEN SAUCE

Preparation: 40 minutes
Cooking: 3 hours
Chilling: 4 hours
Serves: 6

• 6 leeks
• 6 beetroot leaves
• 4 stems celery
• 40 g (1½ oz) butter
• 1 chicken, about 1.5 kg (3½ lb)
• bunch fresh flat-leaf parsley
• salt and pepper
• 3 egg yolks
• 25 cl (8 fl oz) Yoplait crème fraîche gastronomique

Sauce:
• 1 sprig fresh tarragon
• 2 sprigs fresh chervil
• 2 sprigs fresh flat-leaf parsley
• 10 cl (3½ fl oz) Yoplait crème fraîche light
• 1 Yoplait natural yogurt
• salt and pepper

• Clean the vegetables and slice them.
• Melt the butter in a large pan. Add the vegetables and cook for 1 to 2 minutes. Add the chicken, parsley, seasoning to taste and sufficient water to three-quarters cover the chicken. Cover and bring to the boil; simmer for 2 hours.
• Drain the chicken, remove the skin and bones and pull the flesh into small pieces. Strain the chicken stock, reserving the stock and vegetables. Blend the vegetables in a food processor with one ladleful of the chicken stock.
• Preheat the oven to 180°C (350°F, Gas Mark 4).
• Beat the egg yolks with the crème fraîche, puréed vegetables, pieces of chicken and seasoning to taste. Mix well.
• Butter a terrine generously. Add the chicken mixture, smoothing the surface. Cover with a piece of greased foil or parchment. Stand in a roasting tin and add sufficient hot water to come halfway up the sides of the terrine. Cook for 45 minutes.
• Leave to cool and then chill for 4 hours.
For the sauce:
• Finely chop the herbs. Mix the crème fraîche with the yogurt and add seasoning to taste. Stir in the herbs. Chill the sauce.
• Serve the terrine accompanied by the sauce.

Wine: A fruity red, such as a Cahors.

RABBIT AND ROSEMARY TERRINE

Preparation: 40 minutes
Marinating: 2 hours
Cooking: 2 hours
Chilling: 50 minutes
Serves: 6

• 1 oven-ready rabbit
• 2 medium onions
• 3 cloves garlic
• 1 sprig fresh rosemary
• 2 tomatoes
• 200 ml (6½ fl oz) dry white wine
• salt and pepper
• 3 egg yolks
• 25 cl (8 fl oz) Yoplait crème fraîche
• 30 g (1 oz) butter

• Bone the rabbit and cut the flesh into small pieces. Peel and slice the onions and the garlic. Chop the rosemary.
• Blanch the tomatoes in boiling water for 30 seconds, remove the skins and the seeds and chop the flesh.
• Mix the rabbit with the onions, garlic, chopped tomato, rosemary, wine and seasoning to taste. Mix well and leave to marinate for 2 hours.
• Preheat the oven to 190°C (375°F, Gas Mark 5).
• Beat the egg yolks with the crème fraîche and mix with the rabbit and its marinade. Add extra seasoning if liked.
• Generously butter a large terrine and add the rabbit mixture. Cover with a piece of greased foil or parchment. Stand in a roasting tin and add sufficient hot water to come halfway up the sides of the terrine. Cook for 50 minutes.
• Leave to cool and then chill for 4 hours. Serve with hot toast.

Wine: A fruity red Côtes de Provence.

EELS IN WHITE WINE SAUCE

Preparation: 30 minutes
Cooking: 40 minutes
Serves: 4

• 1 kg (2 lb) eel
• 10 small new onions
• 3 onions
• 2 medium carrots
• 30 g (1 oz) butter
• 3 tablespoons groundnut oil
• 1 bouquet garni
• 1 litre (1¾ pints) dry white wine
• 20 cl (6½ fl oz) Yoplait crème fraîche
• salt and pepper

• Skin and wash the eel; cut it into even-sized pieces. Wash the small onions. Peel and slice the large onions and the carrots.
• Heat the butter and oil in a pan, add the sliced onions and carrots and cook for 3 minutes. Add the pieces of eel and cook quickly until golden. Add the bouquet garni and white wine and bring to the boil; simmer for 15 minutes.
• Remove the pieces of eel and keep warm. Reduce the cooking liquid by half. Stir in the crème fraîche and seasoning to taste. Return the pieces of eel to the sauce and add the small onions. Cook for a further 10 minutes over a gentle heat.
• Serve with fresh noodles.

Wine: A white Graves or perhaps a Pinot Grigio.

FILLETS OF PIKE WITH SAUERKRAUT

Preparation: 20 minutes
Cooking: 30 minutes
Serves: 4

• 1 pike, about 1.5 kg (3½ lb)
• 3 shallots
• 40 g (1½ oz) butter
• 100 ml (3½ fl oz) dry white wine
• 1 kg (2 lb) sauerkraut
• 12.5 cl (4½ fl oz) Yoplait crème fraîche
• salt and pepper

• Preheat the oven to 190°C (375°F, Gas Mark 5).
• Remove the fillets from the fish and cut each one in half. Peel and slice the shallots.
• Melt the butter in a pan and fry the shallots for 2 minutes. Add the wine and reduce by one-third. Add the sauerkraut and crème fraîche and cook for 5 minutes.
• Place half the sauerkraut in a shallow ovenproof dish, lay the pike fillets on top, season to taste and cover with the remaining sauerkraut. Cover with greased foil or parchment. Bake in the oven for 20 minutes.
• Serve with boiled or steamed new potatoes.

Wine: An Alsace white, such as a Gewürztraminer.

SQUID WITH TOMATO FONDUE

Preparation: 40 minutes
Cooking: 50 minutes
Serves: 4

- 1 kg (2lb) squid
- 1 kg (2 lb) tomatoes
- 2 onions
- 2 cloves
- 4 sprigs fresh flat-leaf parsley
- 100 g (3½ oz) butter
- 100 ml (3½ fl oz) dry white wine
- 100 ml (3½ fl oz) fish stock
- 2 pinches cayenne pepper
- salt and pepper
- 20 cl (6½ fl oz) Yoplait crème fraîche light

- Clean the squid thoroughly and cut into pieces. Blanch the tomatoes in boiling water for 30 seconds, remove skin and pips and chop the flesh. Peel and slice the onions and garlic, and chop the parsley.
- Melt 60 g (2 oz) of the butter in a pan and cook the onions for 2 minutes. Add the tomato flesh, garlic and parsley and cook for 10· minutes. Add the wine, fish stock, cayenne and seasoning to taste; simmer gently for 20 minutes.
- Melt the remaining butter in a pan, add the squid and cook for 2 minutes. Add the prepared tomato fondue and cook gently for a further 10 minutes. Stir in the crème fraîche, heat through for a minute or two and adjust seasoning to taste.
- Serve with boiled or steamed rice.

Wine: A lightish red Burgundy or a rosé with a fairly good depth of flavour.

TROUT BRAISED WITH SHALLOTS

Preparation: 20 minutes
Cooking: 25 minutes
Serves: 4

- 2 trout, about 400 g (14 oz) each
- salt and pepper
- 6 button mushrooms
- 8 shallots
- 100 ml (3½ fl oz) dry white wine
- 40 g (1½ oz) butter
- 20 cl (6½ fl oz) Yoplait crème fraîche gastronomique

- Preheat the oven to 190°C (375°F, Gas Mark 5).
- Remove the fillets from each fish and season them. Wash, dry and slice the mushrooms. Peel and slice the shallots.
- Place the mushrooms and shallots in a greased shallow ovenproof dish. Arrange the trout fillets on top. Moisten with the wine, add small knobs of butter and seasoning to taste. Bake in the oven for 20 minutes.
- Remove the trout fillets and keep warm. Stir the crème fraîche into the cooking juices and bring to the boil; cook gently for 5 minutes.
- Arrange the fish on warmed serving plates and spoon over the sauce.

Wine: A good, crisp dry white or a well-chilled Extra Dry Noilly Prat.

SCALLOPS WITH SWEETBREADS

Preparation: 30 minutes
Cooking: 20 minutes
Serves: 4

- 12 scallops, shelled
- 3 shallots
- 2 spring onions
- 500 g (1 lb) sweetbreads
- 80 g (2¾ oz) butter
- 100 ml (3½ fl oz) dry white wine
- 10 cl (3½ fl oz) Yoplait crème fraîche
- 100 ml (3½ fl oz) milk
- salt and pepper
- 5 fresh chives, snipped

- Clean the scallops and cut them in half horizontally. Peel and slice the shallots and the onions. Clean the sweetbreads and cut them into escalopes.
- Melt half the butter in a pan, add the sweetbreads and fry for 3 minutes on each side. Remove from the pan and keep warm.
- Melt the remaining butter, add the shallots and onions and cook for 2 minutes. Remove from the pan and keep warm. Add the scallops to the same pan and cook for 2 minutes. Remove and keep warm.
- Add the wine to the pan and reduce by half. Stir in the crème fraîche and milk and bring to the boil. Add seasoning to taste. Add the scallops, sweetbreads and onions to sauce and heat through for 30 seconds.
- Spoon on to serving plates and sprinkle with snipped chives.

Wine: A full, fruity white, such as Puligny Montrachet, or a 'New World' Chardonnay.

FLAMBEED LANGOUSTINE TAILS

Preparation: 40 minutes
Cooking: 20 minutes
Serves: 4

- 2¼ kg (5 lb) shell-on langoustines
- 2 shallots
- 1 medium carrot
- 2 tomatoes
- 30 g (1 oz) butter
- 50 ml (2 fl oz) Cognac
- 20 cl (6½ fl oz) Yoplait crème fraîche gastronomique
- 2 pinches cayenne pepper
- salt and pepper

- Shell the langoustines, removing heads and tails. Peel and slice the shallots and carrot. Blanch the tomatoes in boiling water for 30 seconds. Remove the skins and pips, and chop the flesh.
- Melt the butter in a large shallow pan, add the shallots and carrot and cook for 3 minutes. Add the langoustines and cook for a further 2 minutes.
- Flame the Cognac in a metal ladle or small pan and carefully pour over the langoustines. Once the flames die down, add the crème fraîche, cayenne and seasoning to taste. Cook for 10 minutes over a gentle heat. Add the chopped tomato and cook for a further 5 minutes.
- Serve with boiled or steamed rice.

Wine: A white with a good bouquet, such as a Mâcon.

BASS WITH MUSHROOMS

Preparation: 20 minutes
Cooking: 30 minutes
Serves: 4

• 2 shallots
• 500 g (1 lb) button mushrooms
• 1 bass, about 1 kg (2 lb)
• 40 g (1½ oz) butter
• 100 ml (3½ fl oz) fish stock
• 25 cl (8 fl oz) Yoplait crème fraîche gastronomique
• salt and pepper
• juice of 1 lemon
• 2 sprigs fresh chervil

• Preheat the oven to 190°C (375°F, Gas Mark 5).
• Peel and slice the shallots. Wash, dry and slice the mushrooms. Remove the fillets from the bass; wipe them carefully.
• Melt the butter in a shallow ovenproof dish, add the shallots and cook for 1 to 2 minutes. Stir in the stock and the crème fraîche and reduce by one-third. Add half the mushrooms and arrange the fish fillets on top. Finally cover with the remaining mushrooms. Season to taste, squeeze over the lemon juice and add the sprigs of chervil.
• Bake in the oven for 20 minutes, then serve with fresh noodles or new potatoes.

Wine: A 'floral' white such as Entre-Deux-Mers.

PAPILLOTES OF POLLACK AND YOUNG VEGETABLES

Preparation: 30 minutes
Cooking: 15 minutes
Serves: 4

• 800 g (1¾ lb) pollack
• 4 spring onions
• 200 g (7 oz) haricot verts (fine green beans)
• salt and pepper
• 2 new carrots
• pinch cayenne pepper
• 20 cl (6½ fl oz) Yoplait crème fraîche gastronomique
• several small sprigs fresh chervil

• Preheat the oven to 200°C (400°F, Gas Mark 6).
• Divide the pollack into four equal pieces. Clean the onions and slice them thinly, including their green tops. Top and tail the haricots verts. Blanch them in boiling salted water for 5 minutes; drain thoroughly. Scrape the carrots and cut them into very fine strips.
• Cut four rectangles of foil, about 23 × 20 cm (9 × 8 inches). Place a piece of pollack on one half of each piece of foil. Add the prepared vegetables, salt, pepper and cayenne to taste, a little crème fraîche and a few sprigs of chervil. Fold the foil over the fish and pinch the edges together to seal. Place on a baking sheet and cook in the oven for 15 minutes.
• Serve with boiled rice, or tiny new potatoes, and a salad.

Wine: A lightish, but rounded, white Burgundy, such as Aligoté.

MONKFISH WITH RED PEPPERS

Preparation: 15 minutes
Cooking: 40 minutes
Serves: 4

- 3 red peppers
- 2 cloves garlic
- 20 cl (6½ fl oz) Yoplait crème fraîche
- salt and pepper
- 40 g (1½ oz) butter
- 1 monkfish tail, about 1.25 kg (2½ lb)
- 100 ml (3½ fl oz) fish stock

- Preheat the oven to 200°C (400°F, Gas Mark 6).
- Wrap each pepper in foil and bake in the oven for 20 minutes. Open the foil and allow the peppers to cool slightly. Remove the skin and the seeds, and cut the flesh of two of the peppers into strips.
- Place the remaining red pepper in the bowl of a food processor with the peeled garlic and blend until smooth.
- Mix the red pepper purée with the crème fraîche and seasoning to taste.
- Melt the butter in a large deep sauté pan, add the monkfish and cook over a moderate heat until golden on all sides. Add the fish stock and reduce by half. Add the strips of pepper and the red pepper cream. Cover and cook over a gentle heat for 10 minutes.
- Serve with fresh noodles or with a creamy purée of potatoes.

Wine: A spicy rosé is excellent with this dish – a complement to the peppers.

SKATE WITH CREAM SAUCE

Preparation: 20 minutes
Cooking: 15 minutes
Serves: 4

- 1 kg (2 lb) skate
- salt and pepper
- 100 g (3½ oz) butter
- 25 cl (8 fl oz) Yoplait crème fraîche gastronomique
- 2 egg yolks
- juice of ½ lemon
- several sprigs fresh chervil

- Wash the skate. Place it in a large pan with about 2 litres (3½ pints) water and seasoning to taste. Bring to the boil and simmer for 15 minutes. Drain the skate and remove the skin. Place the skate in a shallow ovenproof dish and keep warm.
- Melt the butter in a small pan until melted and just bubbling. Remove from the heat and beat in the egg yolks and crème fraîche to give a smooth 'satiny' sauce. Season to taste, add the lemon juice and pour immediately over the hot fish.
- Garnish with chervil and serve with plain boiled or steamed potatoes.

Wine: A flowery, honeyed white wine, such as Jasnières, or a light Australian or Italian Chardonnay.

WHITING WITH MUSTARD SAUCE

Preparation: 30 minutes
Cooking: 30 minutes
Serves: 4

• 1 large piece of crepine*
• 1 medium onion
• 1 medium carrot
• 40 g (1½ oz) butter
• 50 ml (2 fl oz) dry white wine
• salt and pepper
• 100 ml (3½ fl oz) fish stock
• 20 cl (6½ fl oz) Yoplait crème fraîche gastronomique
• 8 thin slices streaky bacon
• 2 tablespoons Meaux mustard
• several sprigs fresh chervil

• Preheat the oven to 225°C (425°F, Gas Mark 7).
• Rinse the crepine and cut it into four pieces. Peel and slice the onion and carrot.
• Melt half the butter in a pan, add the onion and carrot and cook over a gentle heat for 5 minutes, stirring from time to time. Add the white wine and reduce by a half. Season to taste and stir in the fish stock and crème fraîche.
• Lay each piece of crepine on a clean work surface and place two slices of bacon and a fish fillet on top of each one. Spread with mustard and roll up, enclosing the fish in the crepine. Place the fish in a buttered, shallow ovenproof dish and bake in the oven for 10 minutes. Reduce the temperature to 190°C (375°F, Gas Mark 5), spoon over the sauce and return to the oven for 10 minutes.
• Garnish with chervil and serve with an olive oil potato purée.

Wine: Something white, crisp and fruity, such as Gros Plant.

* Crepine, or crepinette as it is sometimes called, is the lining of the pig's stomach, used for wrapping delicate savoury foods prior to cooking. Ask your butcher for it.

ROCK SALMON WITH GARLIC CREAM

Preparation: 30 minutes
Cooking: 25 minutes
Serves: 4

• 4 tomatoes
• 2 medium onions
• 40 g (1½ oz) butter
• 1 kg (2 lb) rock salmon, cut into portions
• 2 tablespoons chopped fresh parsley
• salt and pepper
• 100 ml (3½ fl oz) dry white wine
• Garlic Cream (page 10)

• Blanch the tomatoes in boiling water for 30 seconds and remove the skins. Scoop out the centre seeds and chop the flesh.
• Peel and slice the onions. Melt the butter in a pan and cook the onions for 4 minutes. Remove the onions and keep on one side.
• Add the fish portions to the butter in the pan and sauté quickly on both sides. Add the onions, tomatoes, parsley, seasoning to taste and the wine. Cook gently for 20 minutes.
• While the fish is cooking, prepare the garlic cream.
• Remove the fish from the pan and place on warm serving plates. Remove the bones, if wished.
• Blend the garlic cream into the fish pan juices and cook for 1 minute. Spoon the sauce over the fish and serve with fresh pasta or lightly boiled new potatoes.

Wine: A white with a good floral bouquet, or a Provençal rosé.

JOHN DORY WITH SORREL

Preparation: 40 minutes
Cooking: 25 minutes
Serves: 4

- 3 shallots
- 100 g (3½ oz) butter
- 250 ml (8 fl oz) dry white wine
- 2 John Dory, about 500 g (1 lb) each, filleted
- 1 kg (2 lb) spinach
- 400 g (14 oz) sorrel
- 1 tablespoon flour
- 10 cl (3½ fl oz) Yoplait crème fraîche
- 100 ml (3½ fl oz) milk
- salt and pepper
- 3 egg yolks
- juice of ½ lemon

- Preheat the oven to 200°C (400°F, Gas Mark 6).
- Peel and chop the shallots. Heat 20 g (¾ oz) of the butter in a large shallow pan and cook the shallots for 2 minutes. Add the white wine and bring to simmering point. Add the John Dory fillets and poach gently for 3 minutes. Drain the fish and reserve the cooking juices.
- Remove the stalks from the spinach and sorrel. Wash both greens and shake dry. Melt 30 g (1 oz) of the butter in a pan and add the sorrel; cook for 2 minutes. Blanch the spinach in boiling salted water for 2 minutes; drain well. Mix the sorrel and spinach in a pan with the flour and cook gently until all excess moisture has evaporated. Add the crème fraîche, milk and seasoning to taste; keep warm.
- Reduce the fish cooking juices. Remove the pan from the heat and beat in the egg yolks, the rest of the butter (cut into small pieces) and the lemon juice, to give a light, creamy sauce.
- Place the spinach and sorrel in a layer in a greased gratin dish and arrange the fish fillets on top. Spoon the sauce over evenly. Cook in the oven for 10 minutes.

Wine: A good Chablis, or other well-rounded white wine.

FILLETS OF SOLE WITH ARTICHOKES

Preparation: 15 minutes
Cooking: 15 minutes
Serves: 4

- 3 shallots
- 8 artichoke bottoms
- 80 g (2¾ oz) butter
- 50 ml (2 fl oz) dry white wine
- 20 cl (6½ fl oz) Yoplait crème fraîche light
- salt and pepper
- 2 pinches cayenne pepper
- 12 single fillets of sole, skinned
- sprigs fresh chervil

- Peel and slice the shallots. Chop the artichoke bottoms.
- Melt 20 g (¾ oz) of the butter in a pan and cook the shallots for a few minutes. Add the wine and reduce by a quarter. Add the artichokes and crème fraîche and cook gently for 5 minutes. Season to taste with salt, pepper and cayenne.
- Melt the remaining butter in a large, non-stick frying pan, add the sole fillets and cook for 2 minutes on the first side and 1 minute on the second.
- Arrange the sole fillets on warm serving plates, spoon the sauce over evenly and garnish with sprigs of chervil.

Wine: A fruity Loire wine, well chilled.

FRICASSEE OF SOLE WITH CEPES

Preparation: 30 minutes
Cooking: 30 minutes
Serves: 4

- 3 shallots
- 1 medium onion
- 3 cloves garlic
- 12 fillets sole, skinned
- 1 kg (2 lb) cèpe mushrooms
- 2 tablespoons peanut oil
- 80 g (2¾ oz) butter
- 2 tablespoons chopped fresh parsley
- salt and pepper
- 20 cl (6½ fl oz) Yoplait crème fraîche gastronomique
- sprigs fresh flat-leaf parsley

- Peel and slice the shallots, onion and garlic. Cut the sole into 'goujons' – thin diagonal strips. Clean the cèpes and slice them.
- Heat the oil and half the butter in a pan, add the cèpes and cook over a moderate heat for 10 minutes. Add the garlic, shallots, onion, chopped parsley and seasoning; cook gently for a further 15 minutes.
- Melt the remaining butter in a large non-stick pan. Add the goujons of sole and cook until pale golden. Season to taste and keep warm.
- Add the crème fraîche to the butter in the pan and bring to the boil; cook for 2 minutes and season to taste.
- Arrange the cèpes and sole on four warm plates. Spoon over the sauce and garnish with parsley leaves.

Wine: A fruity Sauvignon blanc.

PAUPIETTES OF SOLE AND SALMON

Preparation: 40 minutes
Cooking: 30 minutes
Serves: 4

- 500 g (1 lb) fresh salmon
- 1 medium carrot
- 2 shallots
- 2 sprigs fresh coriander
- salt and pepper
- 20 cl (6½ fl oz) Yoplait crème fraîche
- 20 g (¾ oz) butter
- 100 ml (3½ fl oz) dry white wine
- 100 ml (3½ fl oz) fish stock
- 4 sole, skinned and filleted
- pinch cayenne pepper

- Remove the skin and bones from the salmon; chop the flesh. Peel and coarsely chop the carrot. Peel and slice the shallots.
- Place the salmon in a food processor with the coriander, half the shallots and seasoning to taste. Blend until smooth. Add 5 cl (2 fl oz) crème fraîche; blend once again.
- Preheat the oven to 190°C (375°F, Gas Mark 5).
- Carefully stretch the fillets of sole. Lay the fillets on the work surface in pairs, with one fillet slightly overlapping the other. Put some of the salmon mixture in the centre; fold up the fish fillets so as to enclose salmon. Secure with wooden cocktail sticks.
- Melt the butter in a pan, add the remaining shallots and the carrot and cook for 2 minutes. Add the wine and stock and reduce by a half. Spoon the drained shallot and carrot into a greased gratin dish and arrange the fish paupiettes on top. Add the remaining crème fraîche and cayenne to the butter juices from the vegetables, adjusting the seasoning if necessary. Spoon the sauce over the fish. Bake for 20 minutes.
- Serve with a green vegetable.

Wine: A flowery, 'buttery' white wine, such as Meursault.

PORK FILLET EN CROUTE

Preparation: 1 hour
Cooking: 1 hour
Serves: 4

- 3 shallots
- 1 medium onion
- 400 g (14 oz) button mushrooms
- 60 g (2 oz) butter
- 2 pork fillets
- 300 g (10 oz) puff pastry
- salt and pepper
- 3 egg yolks
- 20 cl (6½ fl oz) Yoplait crème fraîche

- Peel and slice the shallots and onion. Wipe the mushrooms with a damp cloth and slice them.
- Melt 30 g (1 oz) of the butter in a large shallow frying pan, add the shallots and onion and cook for 3 minutes. Add the mushrooms and cook over a gentle heat for 10 minutes. Drain the vegetables, reserving their cooking juices.
- Cook the pork fillets in the remaining butter until golden on all sides.
- Preheat the oven to 200°C (400°F, Gas Mark 6).
- Cut the pastry into two equal pieces and roll each one out to form a rectangle, large enough to enclose pork fillets. Lay a pork fillets down the centre of each piece of pastry, add the onion and mushrooms and season to taste. Dampen the pastry edges and fold the pastry over the pork and vegetables, so as to enclose them completely. Pinch the edges to seal and place on a dampened baking sheet. Make a small hole in the top of the pastry and fix with a small greaseproof paper chimney.
- Mix one of the egg yolks with 2 tablespoons of water; glaze the pastry. Mix the remaining egg yolks with the crème fraîche and seasoning. Carefully pour the mixture through the paper chimney. Bake in the oven for 40 minutes.
- Serve piping hot with a tossed salad.

Wine: A light, elegant red, such as a Chinon.

FRICASSEE OF PORK WITH BANANAS

Preparation: 20 minutes
Cooking: 1 hour
Serves: 4

- 3 medium onions
- 1 kg (2 lb) pork fillet
- 40 g (1½ oz) butter
- salt and pepper
- 4 bananas
- grated zest of 1 orange
- 2 tablespoons desiccated coconut
- 2 pinches cayenne pepper
- 10 cl (3½ fl oz) Yoplait crème fraîche
- 100 ml (3½ fl oz) milk

- Peel and slice the onions. Cut the meat into even-sized pieces.
- Melt the butter in a pan, add the meat and cook to seal on all sides. Remove the meat and keep on one side. Add the onions to the butter in the pan and cook until golden. Return the meat to the pan and season to taste. Cover and cook gently for 40 minutes.
- Peel the bananas and cut into 2.5 cm (1 inch) pieces. Add the banana, orange zest, coconut, cayenne, crème fraîche and milk to the meat. Simmer over a gentle heat, uncovered, for 15 minutes.
- Serve with boiled or steamed rice.

Wine: A fruity white wine – one with a hint of citrus.

ROAST PORK WITH APPLES

Preparation: 30 minutes
Cooking: 1 hour
Serves: 4

• 3 onions
• 40 g (1½ oz) butter
• pork tenderloin joint, about 1.25 kg (2¾ lb)
• salt and pepper
• 100 ml (3½ fl oz) cider
• 4 Golden Delicious apples
• juice of ½ lemon
• 2 pinches ground cinnamon
• 20 cl (6½ fl oz) Yoplait crème fraîche

• Peel and slice the onions.
• Melt the butter in a pan over a moderate heat and brown the pork joint on all sides. Remove the pork and keep on one side. Add the onions to the butter in the pan and cook for 3 minutes. Return the pork to the pan, season to taste and add the cider. Cover and cook over a gentle heat for 30 minutes.
• Peel the apples and brush them with lemon juice to prevent them from discolouring. Core the apples and cut them into quarters. Add the apples and cinnamon to the pork and continue cooking for further 10 minutes. Add the crème fraîche and cook, uncovered, for 15 minutes. Adjust seasoning if necessary.
• Serve with baked jacket potatoes.

Wine: A red with a good body, such as Mâcon Villages or a Beaujolais.

PORK AND POTATO TOURTE

Preparation: 20 minutes
Marinating: 24 hours
Cooking: 1½ hours
Serves: 4

• 400 g (14 oz) lean boned pork
• 1 shallot
• 1 good-sized sprig fresh thyme
• 1 bay leaf
• 200 ml (6½ fl oz) dry white wine
• salt and pepper
• 30 g (1 oz) butter
• 2 medium onions
• 500 g (1 lb) potatoes
• 450 g (scant 1 lb) puff pastry
• 20 cl (6½ fl oz) Yoplait crème fraîche gastronomique
• beaten egg

• Cut the meat into small pieces. Peel and slice the shallot. Place the meat, shallot, thyme, bay leaf and white wine in a large shallow dish; season to taste. Cover and chill for 24 hours.
• Preheat the oven to 190°C (375°F, Gas Mark 5).
• Drain the meat. Melt the butter in a large shallow pan and seal the meat on all sides.
• Peel the onions and slice into thin rings. Peel the potatoes and cut into fine slices.
• Roll out two-thirds of the pastry and use to line a 20 cm (8 inch) spring-form cake tin. Arrange the potatoes, onions and meat in alternate layers. Season each layer and spoon the crème fraîche over the top. Moisten the exposed pastry rim.
• Roll out the remaining pastry and lay over the filling. Trim off the excess pastry and pinch the pastry edges together to seal. Make a small hole in the top of the pastry and fix with a small paper funnel. Glaze pastry with beaten egg.
• Bake in the oven for 1½ hours. If the pastry starts to become too brown, cover with greaseproof paper or foil and reduce the oven temperature.
• Serve hot with a crisp salad.

Wine: A fairly full-flavoured white Chardonnay.

WHITE VEAL CASSEROLE

Preparation: 35 minutes
Cooking: 2 hours
Serves: 4

- 2 medium carrots
- 2 cloves garlic
- 2 medium onions
- 2 cloves
- 1 kg (2 lb) boned shoulder of veal, cut into pieces
- 200 ml (6½ fl oz), dry white wine
- bouquet garni
- salt and pepper
- 50 g (1¾ oz) butter
- 50 g (1¾ oz) flour
- 5 cl (2 fl oz) Yoplait crème fraîche
- 50 ml (2 fl oz) milk
- juice of ½ lemon
- 2 egg yolks

- Peel the carrots, garlic and onions. Spike each onion with a clove.
- Place the meat in a large heavy-based pan with the wine, carrots, garlic, onions, bouquet garni and salt and pepper to taste. Add sufficient water to cover. Bring to the boil, cover and simmer gently for 1½ hours.
- Towards the end of cooking, melt the butter in a small pan. Stir in the flour over the heat for 30 seconds. Gradually add 600 ml (1 pint) of the veal cooking liquid, stirring continuously. Drain the veal and add the meat to the sauce with the crème fraîche and milk. Cover and simmer for 20 minutes.
- Just before serving, spoon the meat into a serving dish and keep warm. Mix the lemon juice with the egg yolks and whisk into the sauce. Spoon over the veal and serve immediately.

Wine: A well-chilled, fruity rosé.

ESCALOPES OF VEAL WITH SMOKED HAM

Preparation: 20 minutes
Cooking: 5 minutes
Serves: 4

- 1 clove garlic
- 2 shallots
- 10 good-sized basil leaves
- 4 escalopes of veal
- 4 thin slices Parma ham
- 40 g (1½ oz) butter
- 20 cl (6½ fl oz) Yoplait crème fraîche
- salt and pepper

- Peel the garlic and the shallots. Wash and dry six of the basil leaves. Place the garlic, shallot and basil in the bowl of a food processor and blend to a purée.
- Cut the veal into small 'escalopines'; cut the ham into pieces of the same size. Put a little basil purée on to each piece of ham, top with a piece of veal and roll up, securing with wooden cocktail sticks.
- Melt the butter in a large shallow pan, add the escalopines and cook for 3 minutes over a moderate heat. Turn the meat and cook for a further 2 minutes. Remove the escalopines and keep warm.
- Add the crème fraîche to the sediment in the pan and bring to the boil. Season to taste.
- Spoon the veal on to warm serving plates and spoon the sauce evenly over the top. Garnish with the remaining basil leaves and serve with fresh noodles or asparagus.

Wine: A light Beaujolais or a fruity rosé.

FILLET OF VEAL WITH PLEUROTE MUSHROOMS

Preparation: 30 minutes
Cooking: 1½ hours
Serves: 4

- 6 cloves garlic
- 2 medium onions
- one joint lean, tender veal, about 1.25 kg (2½ lb)
- 1 kg (2 lb) pleurote mushrooms (or chanterelles)
- 40 g (1½ oz) butter
- 1 tablespoon peanut oil
- 100 ml (3½ fl oz) dry white wine
- salt and pepper
- 4 sprigs fresh chervil
- 15 cl (5 fl oz) Yoplait crème fraîche light

- Peel the garlic and the onions. Keep four cloves garlic whole. Slice the remaining garlic and onions, separately. Stud the veal joint with the whole garlic cloves. Clean the mushrooms.
- Heat the butter and oil in a large pan, add the veal joint and brown on all sides; remove the veal. Add the sliced onions and cook for a few minutes until golden. Return the meat to the pan and add the wine and seasoning. Cover and simmer for 1 hour.
- Add the mushrooms, sliced garlic and chervil. Continue cooking for 20 minutes. Stir in the crème fraîche and cook over a gentle heat, uncovered, for a further 10 minutes. Adjust seasoning to taste.

Wine: A red, such as Faugères or Fitou.

ESCALOPES OF VEAL WITH LEEKS

Preparation: 30 minutes
Cooking: 25 minutes
Serves: 4

- 2 medium onions
- 2 cloves garlic
- 4 leeks
- 60 g (2 oz) butter
- 1.25 kg (2½ lb) tiny veal escalopes, (not too thin)
- 1 pinch cayenne pepper
- 250 ml (8 fl oz) beer
- salt and pepper
- 20 cl (6½ fl oz) Yoplait crème fraîche gastronomique

- Peel and slice the onions and the garlic. Clean the leeks and cut them into fine rings.
- Melt the butter in a large shallow frying pan, add the veal and fry quickly on both sides. Remove the veal and keep on one side. Add the onion, garlic and leeks to the fat in the pan and cook gently for 5 minutes. Return the veal to the pan and add the cayenne, beer and salt and pepper to taste; simmer for 5 minutes. Stir in the crème fraîche and simmer for a further 5 to 10 minutes.
- Serve piping hot with cooked rice or fresh noodles.

Wine: A light, fruity red, such as a Bourgueil.

SAUTE OF LAMB

Preparation: 30 minutes
Cooking: 50 minutes
Serves: 4

- 2 medium onions
- 4 tomatoes
- 2 cloves garlic
- 4 sprigs fresh basil
- 1.25 kg (2½ lb) shoulder of lamb
- 6 large black olives, pitted
- 60 g (2 oz) butter
- salt and pepper
- 15 cl (5 fl oz) Yoplait crème fraîche light

- Peel and slice the onions. Blanch the tomatoes in boiling water for 30 seconds; remove the skins and pips and chop the flesh. Peel and chop the garlic. Wash and dry the basil leaves; chop them coarsely. Cut the meat into even-sized pieces. Finely chop the black olives.
- Melt the butter in a large pan and brown the meat on all sides. Add the onions and cook for 2 minutes. Add the tomatoes, garlic, basil and seasoning to taste. Cook slowly over a gentle heat for 40 minutes, stirring from time to time.
- Add the olives and crème fraîche and continue cooking very gently for a further 5 minutes.
- Serve with potato gnocchi.

Wine: A fruity, 'big' red, such as a Barolo.

TOURNEDOS STEAKS WITH SHALLOT SAUCE

Preparation: 10 minutes
Cooking: 15 minutes
Serves: 4

- 6 shallots
- 60 g (2 oz) butter
- 100 ml (3½ fl oz) dry white wine
- 20 cl (6½ fl oz) Yoplait crème fraîche
- salt and pepper
- 4 lamb tournedos, each about 150 g (5 oz)

- Peel and slice the shallots.
- Melt half the butter in a pan and cook the shallots for 2 minutes. Add the white wine and reduce almost completely. Add the crème fraîche and seasoning to taste. Bring to the boil and simmer over a gentle heat for 5 minutes.
- Melt the remaining butter in a shallow pan, add the tournedos and cook briskly on both sides, until cooked to the desired degree. Remove to serving plates and keep warm.
- Add the crème fraîche to the sediment in the pan and stir over a gentle heat. Spoon the sauce evenly over the tournedos and serve with sauté potatoes.

Wine: A full red with good tannin content, such as a Médoc.

BRAISED ANDOUILLETTES

Preparation: 20 minutes
Cooking: 25 minutes
Serves: 4

• 2 Granny Smith apples
• 4 shallots
• 6 button mushrooms
• 20 g (¾ oz) butter
• 50 ml (2 fl oz) Calvados
• 15 cl (5 fl oz) Yoplait crème fraîche gastronomique
• salt and pepper
• 4 andouillette sausages*

• Preheat the oven to 190°C (375°F, Gas Mark 5).
• Peel and core the apples and cut them into quarters. Peel and slice the shallots. Wipe the mushrooms and cut them into thin slices.
• Melt the butter in a flameproof dish, add the shallots and cook for a minute or two. Add the apples, mushrooms, Calvados, crème fraîche and salt and pepper to taste. Place the dish in the oven for 10 minutes.
• Meanwhile, grill the andouillettes under a moderate heat for 10 minutes. Lay the andouillettes on top of the apples and mushrooms and return to the oven for a further 10 minutes.
• Serve with a green salad, dressed with walnut oil.

Wine: A hearty red, such as a Rioja or a Bulgarian Merlot.

* Andouillettes can be bought from many Continental butchers in the UK. As an alternative, use a coarse, country-style sausage.

VEAL KIDNEYS WITH COARSE-GRAIN MUSTARD

Preparation: 30 minutes
Cooking: 25 minutes
Serves: 4

• 2 shallots
• 400 g (14 oz) button mushrooms
• 20 g (¾ oz) butter
• 4 sprigs fresh chervil
• salt and pepper
• 2 veal kidneys, with their fat
• 15 cl (5 fl oz) Yoplait crème fraîche gastronomique
• 2 tablespoons coarse-grain mustard

• Peel and slice the shallots. Wipe the mushrooms and slice them.
• Melt the butter in a heavy-based pan and cook the mushrooms for a minute or two. Add the shallots and chervil and cook for 10 minutes. Season to taste.
• Remove the fat from the kidneys. Chop the kidneys into pieces. Heat a little of their fat in a frying pan and sauté the kidneys for 20 minutes. Remove the kidneys and keep warm.
• Add the crème fraîche and mustard to the mushrooms and pan juices, and bring to the boil. Simmer for 5 minutes.
• Spoon the kidneys on to warm serving plates and spoon the mushrooms and sauce evenly over the top. Garnish with chervil, and serve with cooked rice.

Wine: Quite a bold red – almost any Burgundy would do.

DUCKLING WITH APPLES

Preparation: 30 minutes
Cooking: 55 minutes
Serves: 4

- 100 g (3½ oz) butter
- 1 duckling, about 1.25 kg (2½ lb)
- salt and pepper
- 5 Granny Smith apples
- 50 ml (2 fl oz) Calvados
- 2 pinches ground cinnamon
- 3 tablespoons raisins
- 20 cl (6½ fl oz) Yoplait crème fraîche gastronomique
- sprigs fresh chervil

- Melt half the butter in a large oval flameproof casserole, add the duckling and brown evenly on all sides. Season to taste, cover and cook over a moderate heat for 50 minutes.
- Meanwhile, peel and core the apples and cut them into quarters. Melt the remaining butter in a pan and cook the apples until golden. Add the Calvados and reduce by half. Sprinkle with cinnamon, add the raisins and crème fraîche and adjust the seasoning. Cook over a gentle heat for 15 minutes.
- Cut the cooked duck into pieces and place on warm serving plates with the apple. Spoon the sauce evenly over the duck and garnish with chervil.

Wine: A really fruity red – a Saint-Emilion or maybe one of the many good Chilean reds.

TURKEY PAUPIETTES WITH LEEKS

Preparation: 40 minutes
Cooking: 45 minutes
Serves: 4

Stuffing:
- 50 ml (2 fl oz) milk
- 50 g (1¾ oz) crustless bread
- 200 g (7 oz) pork sausagemeat
- 3 tablespoons chopped fresh parsley
- 1 egg yolk
- salt and pepper

- 4 large, thin turkey escalopes
- 5 leeks
- 60 g (2 oz) butter
- bouquet garni
- 100 ml (3½ fl oz) dry white wine
- 200 ml (6½ fl oz) chicken stock
- 20 cl (6½ fl oz) Yoplait crème fraîche light

For the stuffing:
- Boil the milk and pour over the bread; mash with a fork. Mix in the sausagemeat, chopped parsley, egg yolk and seasoning.
- Stretch the escalopes on a clean work surface and place a portion of the stuffing in the centre of each one. Roll up the escalopes to enclose the stuffing and tie with fine string.
- Clean the leeks, remove the green parts and keep for use in a soup. Slice the white parts.
- Melt half the butter in a shallow pan and fry the turkey paupiettes until sealed on all sides. Add the bouquet garni, wine, stock and seasoning. Cover and simmer for 30 minutes.
- Melt the remaining butter in a pan and cook the white parts of the leeks until just tender. Add to the paupiettes, together with the crème fraîche and simmer, uncovered, for 15 minutes.
- Serve with fresh pasta or plain, boiled new potatoes.

Wine: One of the 'sunshine reds' from South-West France.

ROAST TURKEY WITH PRUNES

Preparation: 40 minutes
Marinating: 2 hours
Cooking: 45 minutes
Serves: 4

- 24 prunes, pitted
- 100 ml (3½ fl oz) dry white wine
- 1 turkey roast, about 800 g (1¾ lb)
- 3 medium onions
- 50 g (1¾ oz) butter
- salt and pepper
- 20 cl (6½ fl oz) Yoplait crème fraîche gastronomique
- sprigs fresh chervil

- Marinate the prunes in the wine for 2 hours. Drain the prunes, reserving the wine.
- Make twelve deep cuts in the turkey joint and tuck a prune into each one. Peel and slice the onions.
- Melt the butter in a flameproof casserole and cook the onions until golden. Remove the onions and keep on one side. Add the turkey roast to the casserole and brown on all sides. Season to taste and add the onions and wine. Cover and cook over a moderate heat for 30 minutes. Add the remaining prunes and the crème fraîche and continue cooking, covered, for a further 15 minutes.
- Carve the turkey into slices and serve on warm plates with the prunes and onions. Whisk the hot sauce and serve separately. Garnish each portion with chervil.

Wine: A fairly hearty Burgundy.

CHICKEN CURRY

Preparation: 30 minutes
Cooking: 50 minutes
Serves: 4

- 1 chicken, about 1.25 kg (2½ lb)
- 2 medium onions
- 80 g (2¾ oz) butter
- 1 tablespoon curry powder
- 100 ml (3½ fl oz) coconut milk
- salt and pepper
- 2 Granny Smith apples
- 10 cl (3½ fl oz) Yoplait crème fraîche gastronomique
- 3 tablespoons flaked almonds

- Cut the chicken into small joints. Peel and slice the onions.
- Melt half the butter in a deep sauté pan, add the chicken and brown all over. Remove the chicken and keep to one side. Fry the onions for 3 minutes until golden and return the chicken to the pan. Stir in the curry powder and then the coconut milk; add seasoning to taste. Cover and simmer for 30 minutes.
- Meanwhile, peel and core the apples and cut into slices. Melt the remaining butter in a frying pan and fry the apple slices until golden.
- Stir the crème fraîche into the chicken mixture and bring to the boil; simmer for 5 minutes.
- Brown the almonds under the grill on a non-stick baking sheet.
- Spoon the chicken pieces and apple on to warm serving plates and spoon over the sauce. Sprinkle with almonds and serve with rice.

Wine: A Rhine wine, with predominantly sweetish undertones.

CHICKEN WITH LANGOUSTINES

Preparation: 40 minutes
Cooking: 1½ hours
Serves: 4

- 12 langoustines (crayfish)
- 1 tablespoon olive oil
- salt and pepper
- 1 chicken, about 1.25 kg (2½ lb)
- 40 g (1½ oz) butter
- 1 bottle Muscadet
- 3 spring onions
- ½ teaspoon cornflour
- 20 cl (6½ fl oz) Yoplait crème fraîche light

- Shell and de-head the langoustines, taking care to keep the tails intact.
- Heat the oil in a large pan, add the langoustine heads and shells and stir over a brisk heat for a few minutes. Add 1 litre (1¾ pints) water and salt and pepper. Bring to the boil and simmer for 20 minutes. Strain the shellfish stock and reduce by half.
- Cut the chicken into even-sized pieces.
- Melt the butter in a large pan and fry the chicken until sealed on all sides. Remove from the pan and keep on one side. Add the langoustine tails to the butter remaining in the pan and cook for 2 minutes, stirring. Remove the langoustines.
- Return the chicken to the pan and add the Muscadet and reduced shellfish stock. Cook over a gentle heat, uncovered, for 50 minutes.
- Clean the spring onions and slice them.
- Blend the cornflour with 2 tablespoons water and stir into the chicken, together with the crème fraîche. Add the langoustine tails and spring onions, and heat through for a minute or two. Serve with cooked rice.

Wine: A crisp white wine from the Loire.

STUFFED CHICKEN THIGHS WITH CRANBERRIES

Preparation: 40 minutes
Cooking: 40 minutes
Serves: 4

- 4 chicken thighs
- 2 shallots
- 1 small carrot
- 1 medium onion
- 2 chicken breasts, boned and skinned
- 1 egg yolk
- salt and pepper
- 40 g (1½ oz) butter
- 2 tablespoons white wine vinegar
- 1 tablespoon caster sugar
- 1 small jar cranberries
- 20 cl (6½ fl oz) Yoplait crème fraîche light
- small sprigs fresh chervil

- Open the chicken thighs; remove the bones and tendons. Peel the shallots and carrot. Peel and slice the onion.
- Chop the chicken breasts and place in the bowl of a food processor with the carrot, shallots, egg yolk and seasoning to taste. Blend until fairly smooth.
- Stuff the chicken thighs with the stuffing and sew together with a trussing needle and thread.
- Melt the butter in a deep sauté pan, add the chicken thighs and cook until golden on all sides. Add the onion and seasoning to taste. Cover and cook over a gentle heat for 30 minutes. Stir in the vinegar, sugar, drained cranberries and crème fraîche; heat through gently.
- Spoon the chicken thighs on to warm serving plates with the cranberries and spoon over the sauce. Garnish with sprigs of chervil. Serve with rice or florets of broccoli.

Wine: A curranty Californian red.

CHICKEN WITH HERBS

Preparation: 30 minutes
Cooking: 55 minutes
Serves: 4

• 4 sprigs fresh tarragon
• 5 sprigs fresh chervil
• 4 sprigs fresh flat-leaf parsley
• 200 g (7 oz) sorrel
• 2 shallots
• 1 chicken, about 1.25 kg (2½ lb)
• 60 g (2 oz) butter
• salt and pepper
• 100 ml (3½ fl oz) chicken stock
• 20 cl (6½ fl oz) Yoplait crème fraîche

• Wash and dry the herbs. Remove the stalks from the sorrel. Chop all of them coarsely. Peel and slice the shallots. Cut the chicken into even-sized pieces.
• Melt the butter in a pan, add the chicken and cook until golden on all sides. Add the shallots and seasoning and cook for a further 3 minutes. Add the stock and bring to the boil; cover and simmer for 35 minutes.
• Stir in the herbs and crème fraîche and bring to the boil; simmer, uncovered, for 10 minutes.
• Serve with sauté potatoes.

Wine: A spicy red from the Languedoc.

GUINEA FOWL IN BEER

Preparation: 30 minutes
Cooking: 1 hour
Serves: 4

• 4 medium onions
• 2 cloves garlic
• 2 medium carrots
• 8 small waxy potatoes
• 60 g (2 oz) butter
• 1 guinea fowl, cut into serving pieces
• 150 ml (5 fl oz) light beer
• salt and pepper
• 15 cl (5 fl oz) Yoplait crème fraîche gastronomique
• 6 fresh chives, snipped

• Peel and slice the onions and garlic. Peel the carrots and cut into rings. Peel the potatoes.
• Melt the butter in a large pan, add the pieces of guinea fowl and cook for a few minutes until golden on all sides. Remove the guinea fowl and keep on one side. Add the onions, carrots and garlic to the butter in the pan and cook for 3 minutes.
• Return the guinea fowl to the pan and add the beer and salt and pepper to taste. Bring to the boil and simmer gently for 20 minutes. Add the potatoes and continue to cook gently for a further 20 minutes. Stir in the crème fraîche and simmer for a further 10 minutes. Sprinkle with snipped chives before serving.

Wine: A deep red from Chile or Bulgaria, or a light beer.

FRICASSEE OF RABBIT WITH MUSHROOMS

Preparation: 30 minutes
Cooking: 1 hour
Serves: 4

• 1 skinned and prepared rabbit, about 1.25 kg (2½ lb)
• 2 tomatoes
• 3 medium onions
• 2 cloves garlic
• 400 g (14 oz) button mushrooms
• 60 g (2 oz) butter
• 3 tablespoons chopped parsley
• salt and pepper
• 100 ml (3½ fl oz) dry white wine
• 20 cl (6½ fl oz) Yoplait crème fraîche gastronomique

• Cut the rabbit into serving pieces. Blanch the tomatoes in boiling water for 30 seconds, remove the skins and pips and chop the flesh. Peel and slice the onions and garlic. Clean the mushrooms.
• Melt the butter in a deep sauté pan, add the rabbit and cook until golden on all sides. Remove the rabbit and keep on one side. Add the onions to the pan and cook until golden. Stir in the tomatoes, garlic, parsley and seasoning; cook for 5 minutes. Add the rabbit pieces and the wine and simmer gently, covered, for 40 minutes.
• Add the mushrooms and cook, uncovered, for a further 10 minutes. Stir in the crème fraîche and heat through.

Wine: *A really good, golden, white Chardonnay.*

SADDLE OF RABBIT WITH ROSEMARY

Preparation: 30 minutes
Marinating: 2 hours
Cooking: 1 hour
Serves: 4

• 2 saddles of rabbit
• 1 generous sprig fresh rosemary
• 100 ml (3½ fl oz) dry white wine
• salt and pepper
• 3 tomatoes
• 6 baby new onions
• 2 cloves garlic
• 50 g (1¾ oz) butter
• 20 cl (6½ fl oz) Yoplait crème fraîche

• Cut each rabbit saddle in half and spike each piece with tiny sprigs of fresh rosemary. Place in a shallow dish with the white wine and salt and pepper to taste. Cover and marinate in the refrigerator for 2 hours.
• Blanch the tomatoes in boiling water for 30 seconds, remove the skins and seeds and chop the flesh. Peel the onions and cut them into quarters, including the green part. Peel and crush tomatoes and garlic.
• Melt the butter in a deep pan, add the rabbit and seal on all sides. Remove the rabbit and keep on one side. Add the onions to the pan and cook for 2 minutes until golden. Add the tomatoes and garlic, and cook for 10 minutes.
• Return the rabbit to the pan, together with the marinade, and cook gently for 40 minutes, stirring from time to time. Stir in the crème fraîche and heat through.
• Serve with fresh noodles, sauté potatoes or a green vegetable.

Wine: *A white Bordeaux or a light Chardonnay.*

STUFFED QUAIL WITH FIGS

Preparation: 40 minutes
Cooking: 20 minutes
Serves: 4

- 1 shallot
- 8 chicken livers
- 70 g (2½ oz) butter
- salt and pepper
- 8 quails
- 8 rashers streaky bacon
- 16 fresh figs
- 2 pinches ground cinnamon
- 10 cl (3½ fl oz) Yoplait crème fraîche
- 100 ml (3½ fl oz) milk
- 2 tablespoons chopped fresh parsley

- Peel and chop the shallot. Clean the chicken livers.
- Melt just under half the butter in a frying pan, add the chicken livers and shallot and cook for 3 minutes. Place in the bowl of a food processor with seasoning to taste and blend to a purée.
- Stuff each quail with the purée. Lay two bacon rashers over the breast of each bird and tie with fine string.
- Melt the remaining butter in a pan, add the quail and cook on all sides until golden. Cover and cook gently for 10 minutes more.
- Meanwhile, wash the figs, dry them and cut into quarters. Add them to the pan and sprinkle with cinnamon. Cook for 5 minutes. Stir in the crème fraîche and milk and cook gently for a further 5 minutes. Add the parsley and adjust seasoning to taste.
- Serve with young broad beans, mange tout or a selection of new young vegetables.

Wine: A robust red from the South of France, such as a Bandol.

PHEASANT WITH CEPES

Preparation: 40 minutes
Cooking: 1 hour
Serves: 4

- 2 Yoplait petits suisses cheeses
- salt and pepper
- 1 plump oven-ready pheasant
- 2 shallots
- 700 g (1½ lb) cèpes mushrooms
- 100 g (3½ oz) butter
- 2 liqueur glasses of Marc de Bourgogne or Cognac
- 300 ml (½ pint) dry white wine
- 15 cl (5 fl oz) Yoplait crème fraîche gastronomique
- 4 sprigs fresh chervil

- Mash the petits suisses with seasoning to taste and use to stuff the pheasant.
- Peel and slice the shallots. Wipe the cèpes and slice them.
- Melt half the butter in a large frying pan, add the shallots and cèpes and cook for 10 minutes.
- Melt the remaining butter in a deep flameproof casserole, and the pheasant and cook until golden on all sides. Flambé with the Marc or Cognac and then add the white wine and seasoning. Cover and cook gently for 40 minutes.
- Add the cèpes and the crème fraîche and cook, uncovered, for a further 5 minutes. Add the sprigs of chervil and serve with plain boiled new potatoes and small turnips.

Wine: A Pomerol or perhaps a Fitou – something red, with a good body.

WARM COURGETTE MOULD

Preparation: 30 minutes
Cooking: 1 hour
Serves: 4

- 2 kg (4 lb) courgettes
- 4 medium onions
- 50 g (1¾ oz) butter
- salt and pepper
- 3 egg yolks
- 15 cl (5 fl oz) Yoplait crème fraîche
- 1 pinch cayenne pepper

- Top and tail the courgettes. Wash them and cut them into thin slices. Peel and slice the onions.
- Melt 40 g (1½ oz) of the butter in a pan, add the onions and cook for 3 minutes. Add the courgettes and seasoning to taste; cover and cook gently for 20 minutes.
- Preheat the oven to 190°C (375°F, Gas Mark 5).
- Beat the egg yolks with the crème fraîche, cayenne and seasoning to taste. Add the well-drained courgettes and mix well.
- Pour the mixture into a buttered savarin mould. Stand in a roasting tin and add sufficient hot water to come halfway up the sides of the mould. Cook in the oven for 35 minutes. Reduce the temperature to 180°C (350°F, Gas Mark 4) and cook for a further 10 minutes.
- Carefully unmould the savarin and serve warm with a tomato coulis. Delicious, either as a starter or as an accompaniment to cooked meals such as veal.

Wine: A light white, such as a Frascati.

CUCUMBER WITH SAUCE POULETTE

Preparation: 20 minutes
Cooking: 10 minutes
Serves: 4

- 2 cucumbers
- salt and pepper
- 60 g (2 oz) butter
- 1 teaspoon white wine vinegar
- 10 cl (3½ fl oz) Yoplait crème fraîche
- 100 ml (3½ fl oz) milk
- 3 egg yolks

- Peel the cucumbers and cut in half lengthways. Scoop out the centre seeds with a teaspoon. Cut the cucumber flesh into 4 cm (1½ inch) slices. Blanch in boiling salted water for 2 to 3 minutes; drain and dry.
- Melt the butter in a large frying pan, add the cucumber and cook for 3 minutes. Add the vinegar and cook for 30 seconds. Add the crème fraîche, milk and seasoning, and reduce slightly.
- Beat the egg yolks and blend in 2 tablespoons of the cucumber sauce. Add the mixture to the pan and heat through gently. Serve warm with fish or grilled meats.

Wine: Dependent on the accompanying main dish.

CARROT AND TURNIP PUREE

Preparation: 20 minutes
Cooking: 40 minutes
Serves: 4

- 1.5 kg (3¼ lb) carrots
- 400 g (14 oz) turnips
- 2 shallots
- 40 g (1½ oz) butter
- salt and pepper
- sprig fresh chervil
- 1 egg yolk
- 15 cl (5 fl oz) Yoplait crème fraîche light

- Peel the carrots and turnips and cut them into pieces. Peel and chop the shallots.
- Melt the butter in a large pan, add the shallots and cook for 2 minutes. Add the carrots and turnips and sauté for 2 to 3 minutes. Add 1.5 litres (2½ pints) water, seasoning and chervil, bring to the boil and cook over a moderate heat for 30 minutes.
- Drain the vegetables, reserving their cooking liquid and either press them through a mouli or blend them in a food processor. Add a little cooking liquid to give the desired consistency.
- Mix the egg yolk with the crème fraîche and seasoning and beat into the vegetable purée. Warm through over a very gentle heat for 5 minutes.
- Serve as an accompaniment to roast or grilled meats.

Wine: Dependent on the accompanying main dish.

CARROTS WITH CHERVIL CREAM

Preparation: 20 minutes
Cooking: 40 minutes
Serves: 4

- 1.25 kg (2½ lb) carrots
- 2 medium onions
- 2 shallots
- 1 clove garlic
- 5 sprigs fresh chervil
- 40 g (1½ oz) butter
- salt and pepper
- 15 cl (5 fl oz) Yoplait crème fraîche gastronomique

- Peel the carrots and cut into thin rings. Peel and slice the onions, shallots and garlic. Chop the chervil.
- Melt the butter in a pan, add the shallots, onions and garlic and cook over a gentle heat for 4 minutes. Add the carrots and cook for a further 5 minutes, stirring from time to time. Add 100 ml (3½ fl oz) water and seasoning, bring to the boil and cook over a moderate heat for 20 minutes. Stir in the chervil and crème fraîche, and continue cooking over a gentle heat for 10 minutes.
- Delicious with pork or veal, or with poultry.

Wine: Dependent on the accompanying main dish.

CHICORY FONDUE

Preparation: 20 minutes
Cooking: 30 minutes
Serves: 4

- 6 plump heads chicory
- 2 medium onions
- 40 g (1½ oz) butter
- 2 sugar cubes
- salt and pepper
- 50 ml (2 fl oz) chicken stock
- 20 cl (6½ fl oz) Yoplait crème fraîche

- Clean the heads of chicory and slice them. Peel and thinly slice the onions.
- Melt the butter in a heavy-based pan, add the onions and cook for 4 minutes, stirring. Add the chicory, sugar, seasoning and chicken stock; cook, covered, over a gentle heat for 20 minutes.
- Stir in the crème fraîche and cook gently for a further 5 minutes.
- Serve with rabbit, poultry or game, or with boiled gammon.

Wine: Dependent on the accompanying main dish.

FRICASSEE OF BABY PEAS AND ONIONS

Preparation: 30 minutes
Cooking: 30 minutes
Serves: 4

- 800 g (1¾ lb) fresh young peas in their pods
- 225 g (8 oz) tiny new white onions
- 2 shallots
- 1 medium carrot
- 40 g (1½ oz) butter
- 50 ml (2 fl oz) vegetable or chicken stock
- salt and pepper
- 10 cl (3½ fl oz) Yoplait crème fraîche
- 100 ml (3½ fl oz) milk
- 5 fresh chives, snipped

- Shell the peas. Clean the onions and leave them whole. Peel and slice the shallots. Peel the carrot and cut into batons.
- Melt the butter in a pan, add the shallots and onions and cook until pale golden. Add the peas, stock and seasoning; cover and cook for 20 minutes.
- Stir in the crème fraîche and milk, and cook over a moderate heat for a further 5 minutes. Sprinkle with the snipped chives.
- Serve with fish or poultry.

Wine: Dependent on the main dish.

STUFFED ONIONS

Preparation: 40 minutes
Cooking: 30 minutes
Serves: 4

• 3 button mushrooms
• 8 medium onions
• 2 shallots
• 200 g (7 oz) lean pork, minced
• 200 g (7 oz) lean beef, minced
• 100 g (3½ oz) cooked rice
• 1 egg yolk
• salt and pepper
• 40 g (1½ oz) butter
• 100 ml (3½ fl oz) vegetable or chicken stock
• 20 cl (6½ fl oz) Yoplait crème fraîche gastronomique

• Preheat the oven to 200°C (400°F, Gas Mark 6).
• Clean the mushrooms and chop them. Peel the onions and hollow each one out carefully. Peel and slice the shallots.
• Mix the meats with the shallots, rice, mushrooms, egg yolk and seasoning. Stuff the onions with this mixture.
• Butter a gratin dish generously. Stand the onions upright in the dish and spoon over the stock. Cook in the oven for 20 minutes.
• Stir the crème fraîche into the onion juices and cook for a further 10 minutes.

Wine: Dependent on the main dish.

ONION TARTS

Preparation: 30 minutes
Cooking: 20 minutes
Serves: 4

• 3 medium onions
• 2 thin slices smoked ham
• 175 g (6 oz) shortcrust pastry
• 10 cl (3½ fl oz) Yoplait crème fraîche
• 1 egg
• salt and pepper
• 40 g (1½ oz) butter

• Preheat the oven to 200°C (400°F, Gas Mark 6).
• Peel and thinly slice the onions. Cut the ham into slivers.
• Roll out the pastry fairly thinly and cut four circles, each one about 10 to 13 cm (4 to 5 inches) in diameter. Place on a greased baking sheet and pinch up the edges.
• Beat the crème fraîche with the egg and seasoning.
• Melt the butter in a pan, add the onions and cook them until soft, without allowing them to brown. Spread the onions over the pastry circles, sprinkle with ham and spoon over the cream mixture. Bake in the oven for 15 minutes.
• Delicious with roast beef, or with game.

Wine: Dependent on the main dish.

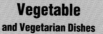

BRAISED LEEKS

Preparation: 20 minutes
Cooking: 35 minutes
Serves: 4

• 12 leeks (white parts only)
• salt and pepper
• 3 shallots
• 50 g (1¾ oz) butter
• 1 tablespoon good mustard
• 20 cl (6½ fl oz) Yoplait crème fraîche

• Preheat the oven to 200°C (400°F, Gas Mark 6).
• Clean the leeks. Blanch them in boiling salted water for 5 minutes and drain them well, pressing gently to extract all excess water. Peel and slice the shallots.
• Melt 20 g (¾ oz) of the butter in a pan, add the shallots and cook for a minute or two. Stir in the mustard and crème fraîche and mix well.
• Grease a gratin dish with a little of the butter. Spooon in half the sauce and arrange the leeks on top. Spoon over the remaining sauce and dot with small knobs of butter. Bake in the oven for 20 minutes.
• Serve with fish, pork or poultry dishes.

Wine: Dependent on the accompanying main dish.

GRATIN OF POTATOES AND MUSHROOMS

Preparation: 30 minutes
Cooking: 1 hour
Serves: 4

• 600 g (1 lb 6 oz) potatoes
• 2 shallots
• 2 cloves garlic
• 400 g (14 oz) button mushrooms
• 125 g (4½ oz) butter
• 3 tablespoons chopped fresh parsley
• salt and pepper
• 2 eggs
• 20 cl (6½ fl oz) Yoplait crème fraîche
• 200 ml (6½ fl oz) milk

• Preheat the oven to 190°C (375°F, Gas Mark 5).
• Peel the potatoes and cut them into thin rounds. Peel and slice the shallots and garlic. Clean the mushrooms and slice them.
• Melt 50 g (1¾ oz) of the butter in a large pan, add the shallots and cook for a minute or two. Add the mushrooms, garlic, parsley and seasoning and cook for 10 minutes.
• Grease a gratin dish with a little of the remaining butter. Arrange the potatoes and mushrooms in alternate layers, seasoning each layer as you go, finishing with a layer of potatoes.
• Beat the eggs with the crème fraîche, milk and seasoning. Pour over the potatoes and dot with knobs of butter. Bake in the oven for 50 minutes. (For a really crusty top, turn the oven up high for the last 10 minutes.)
• Delicious with most savoury main courses, or even on its own.

Wine: Dependent on the accompanying main dish.

POTATO AND CHEESE GRATIN

Preparation: 20 minutes
Cooking: 1 hour
Serves: 4

• 1 kg (2 lb) potatoes
• 1 clove garlic
• 125 g (4½ oz) butter
• 2 eggs
• 10 cl (3½ fl oz) Yoplait crème fraîche
• 400 ml (13 fl oz) milk
• salt and pepper

• Preheat the oven to 190°C (375°F, Gas Mark 5).
• Peel the potatoes and cut them into thin rounds. Peel the garlic, bruise it and rub it around the base and sides of a gratin dish. Grease the dish generously with butter.
• Beat the eggs with the crème fraîche, milk and seasoning to taste.
• Arrange the potatoes in layers in the gratin dish, seasoning each layer. Pour the egg mixture over the potatoes and dot with small knobs of butter. Bake in the oven for 1 hour.
• Serve with roast meats, with cooked ham or, more simply, with a tossed green salad.

Wine: Dependent on the accompanying main dish.

VEGETABLE PUDDING

Preparation: 40 minutes
Cooking: 1 hour
Serves: 4

• 1 medium cauliflower
• salt and pepper
• 50 g (1¾ oz) butter
• 2 medium carrots
• 200 g (7 oz) haricots verts (fine green beans)
• 20 cl (6½ fl oz) Yoplait crème fraîche
• 3 egg yolks
• 30 g (1 oz) Parmesan cheese, grated
• 2 pinches ground nutmeg

• Clean the cauliflower and divide it into florets. Blanch them in boiling salted water for 5 minutes; drain well.
• Melt 30 g (1 oz) of the butter in a pan, and sauté the cauliflower florets for 15 minutes over a gentle heat. Either press them through a mouli or blend them in a food processor.
• Preheat the oven to 180°C (350°F, Gas Mark 4).
• Peel the carrots and cut them into fine batons. Top and tail the haricots verts. Blanch the carrots for 3 minutes and the haricots verts for 2 minutes. Drain well.
• Beat the crème fraîche with the eggs and seasoning to taste. Mix with the cauliflower purée and stir in the carrots and haricots verts.
• Butter a gratin dish generously and spoon in the vegetable mixture; smooth the surface. Dot with knobs of butter and sprinkle with the Parmesan and nutmeg. Cover with a piece of waxed paper and bake in the oven for 40 minutes.
• Delicious with a variety of main dishes.

Wine: Dependent on the accompanying main dish.

BITTER CHOCOLATE MOUSSE

Preparation: 35 minutes
Cooking: 3 minutes
Chilling: 4 hours
Serves: 4

• 250 g (9 oz) dark bitter chocolate
• 2 eggs, separated
• 2 egg yolks
• 10 cl (3½ fl oz) Yoplait crème fraîche
• 100 ml (3½ fl oz) iced water
• 1 sachet vanilla sugar*
• pinch salt

• Break the chocolate into pieces. Place the chocolate in a bowl with 2 tablespoons water; stand over a pan of simmering water and stir until dissolved. Remove the chocolate from the heat and beat in all the egg yolks, one by one.
• Place the crème fraîche, iced water and sugar in a chilled bowl; beat the mixture until thick and fluffy. Keep well chilled.
• Whisk the egg whites to a snow with the pinch of salt.
• Mix the melted chocolate with the whipped crème fraîche and fold in the egg whites lightly but thoroughly. Pour into a serving bowl and chill for 4 hours.
• Serve with sponge fingers or small macaroons.

Wine/Liqueur: Either a sweet dessert wine or a coffee-based liqueur.

*Sachets of vanilla-flavoured sugar are sold in health food shops and good grocers.

MINIATURE CHOCOLATE CHARLOTTES

Preparation: 30 minutes
Cooking: 3 minutes
Chilling: 4 hours
Serves: 8

• 250 g (9 oz) dark bitter chocolate
• 2 eggs, separated
• 2 egg yolks
• 1 piece candied orange peel
• 10 cl (3½ fl oz) Yoplait crème fraîche
• 100 ml (3½ fl oz) iced water
• pinch salt
• langues de chat biscuits

• Break the chocolate into pieces. Place the chocolate in a bowl with 2 tablespoons water; stand over a pan of simmering water and stir until dissolved. Remove the chocolate from the heat and beat in all the egg yolks, one by one. Chop the orange peel finely and add to the chocolate mixture.
• Place the crème fraîche and iced water in a chilled bowl; beat until thick and fluffy. Keep well chilled.
• Whisk the egg whites to a snow with a pinch of salt.
• Mix the melted chocolate with the whipped crème fraîche and lightly but thoroughly fold in the egg whites.
• Line the base and sides of eight ramekins with small langues de chat, cutting them to fit if necessary. Fill with the chocolate mixture. Top with more langues de chat. Chill for 4 hours.
• Unmould carefully on to serving plates. Surround with a pool of light custard.

Wine/Liqueur: Either a sweet dessert wine or a coffee-based liqueur.

CHOCOLATE AND ORANGE FONDANT

Preparation: 20 minutes
Cooking: 30 minutes
Chilling: 4 hours
Serves: 8

• 400 g (14 oz) plain chocolate
• 4 egg yolks
• 20 cl (6½ fl oz) Yoplait crème fraîche gastronomique
• 2 pieces candied orange peel
• 2 tablespoons plump raisins

• Break the chocolate into pieces. Place the chocolate in a bowl; stand over a pan of simmering water and stir until dissolved. Remove the chocolate from the heat and beat in the egg yolks, one by one. Mix with the crème fraîche.
• Chop the orange peel finely. Stir into the chocolate mixture, together with the raisins.
• Spoon into a loaf tin lined with waxed paper. Chill for 4 hours.
• Unmould and cut into slices. Serve each portion with a little crème fraîche flavoured with coffee liqueur.

Wine: Vin de Noix, a French walnut wine.

CHOCOLATE TART

Preparation: 40 minutes
Cooking: 40 minutes
Serves: 6

• 225 g (8 oz) shortcrust pastry
• ½ teaspoon instant coffee
• 200 g (7 oz) plain chocolate
• 4 eggs
• 1 tablespoon rum
• 20 cl (6½ fl oz) Yoplait crème fraîche gastronomique
• 1 sachet vanilla sugar*

• Preheat the oven to 190°C (375°F, Gas Mark 5).
• Roll out the pastry and use to line a loose-bottomed flan tin, about 20 cm (8 inches) in diameter. Press up the edges well. Line with waxed paper and baking beans and bake 'blind' for 15 minutes; remove the paper and beans and bake for a further 15 minutes.
• Dissolve the coffee in 3 tablespoons of water in a bowl. Add the chocolate, broken into pieces; stand over a pan of simmering water and stir until dissolved.
• Beat the eggs with the rum and then beat in the chocolate mixture. Fold in the crème fraîche and vanilla sugar lightly but thoroughly.
• Pour the chocolate mixture into the prepared pastry case and chill until set.

Wine: A good dessert wine, such as Muscat de Beaumes-de-Venise.

* Sachets of vanilla-flavoured sugar are sold in health food shops or good grocers.

CHESTNUT MOUSSE WITH CHOCOLATE SAUCE

Preparation: 20 minutes
Cooking: 3 minutes
Chilling: 4 hours
Serves: 4

• 400 g (14 oz) marrons glacés
• 10 cl (3½ fl oz) Yoplait crème fraîche
• 100 ml (3½ fl oz) iced water
• 2 tablespoons Cognac

Chocolate sauce:
• 300 g (10 oz) plain chocolate
• 5 cl (2 fl oz) Yoplait crème fraîche

• Place the marrons glacés in the bowl of a food processor and blend to a purée.
• Place the crème fraîche and water in a chilled bowl and beat until thick and fluffy. Mix in the chestnut purée and Cognac. Spoon into a serving bowl and chill for 4 hours.
• Break the chocolate into pieces. Place the chocolate in a bowl; stand over a pan of simmering water and stir until dissolved. Cool and then mix in the crème fraîche.
• Serve the chocolate sauce with the mousse.

Wine: A good dessert wine.

ICED MACAROON GATEAU

Preparation: 40 minutes
Cooking: 3 minutes
Freezing: 2 hours
Serves: 6

• 6 macaroons
• 20 cl (6½ fl oz) Yoplait crème fraîche
• 200 ml (6½ fl oz) iced water
• 300 g (10 oz) plain chocolate
• 2 eggs, separated
• 1 egg yolk
• pinch salt

• Place the macaroons in the bowl of a food processor and blend to a powder.
• Place the crème fraîche and iced water in a chilled bowl; beat until thick and fluffy. Lightly mix in the powdered macaroons.
• Break the chocolate into pieces. Place the chocolate in a bowl with 2 tablespoons water; stand over a pan of simmering water and stir until dissolved. Remove the chocolate from the heat and beat in all the egg yolks, one by one.
• Whisk the egg whites to a snow with a pinch of salt. Fold lightly but thoroughly into the chocolate.
• Place half the macaroon mixture in a cake tin lined with waxed paper; smooth the surface level. Add the chocolate mixture in a smooth layer and then top with the remaining macaroon cream. Freeze for 2 hours.

Wine: A Pineau des Charentes, white or rosé.

STRAWBERRY AND ORANGE MOUSSE

Preparation: 30 minutes
Cooking: 1 hour
Chilling: 3 hours
Serves: 4

• 400 g (14 oz) fresh strawberries
• 250 g (9 oz) caster sugar
• 1 orange
• 10 cl (3½ fl oz) Yoplait crème fraîche
• 100 ml (3½ fl oz) iced water

• Wash and drain the strawberries and remove their leafy stalks.
• Place 200 g (7 oz) of the sugar into a pan with 200 ml (6½ fl oz) water; stir over the heat until dissolved. Boil to obtain a syrup. Add the whole strawberries and leave over a very low heat for 1 hour. Drain the strawberries and chill them.
• Thinly pare the rind from the orange and cut into fine matchstick strips. Poach the orange strips with 20 g (¾ oz) of the sugar and 5 tablespoons water over a gentle heat for 15 minutes. Mix the orange strips with the strawberries.
• Place the crème fraîche, water and remaining sugar in a chilled bowl; beat until very thick. Fold in the chilled strawberries. Divide the mousse between four individual serving dishes. Chill for 3 hours.
• Serve with petits fours.

Liqueur: A little Poire William.

RASPBERRY PASTRIES

Preparation: 30 minutes
Cooking: 20 minutes
Serves: 4

• 225 g (8 oz) puff pastry
• 1 egg yolk
• 400 g (14 oz) fresh raspberries
• 30 g (1 oz) caster sugar
• 15 cl (5 fl oz) Yoplait crème fraîche
• 100 ml (3½ fl oz) iced water

• Preheat the oven to 200°C (400°F, Gas Mark 6).
• Roll out the pastry to a thickness of about 5 mm (¼ inch) and cut into four even-sized rectangles. Place on a dampened baking sheet. Beat the egg yolk with 2 tablespoons water; use to glaze the pastry. Bake in the oven for 20 minutes until puffed and golden.
• Meanwhile, place about sixteen of the raspberries in a pan with the sugar, crème fraîche and water. Bring to the boil and press the raspberries to crush them.
• Remove the pastries from the oven. Cut each one in half horizontally. Sandwich the two pieces together on serving plates with raspberries in the centre and spoon the sauce around each pastry. Serve immediately.

Wine/Liqueur: A sparkling Framboise.

RASPBERRY BAVAROIS

Preparation: 40 minutes
Cooking: 10 minutes
Chilling: 4 hours
Serves: 4

- 6 leaves gelatine
- 400 g (14 oz) fresh raspberries
- 500 ml (17 fl oz) milk
- 1 vanilla pod
- 200 g (7 oz) caster sugar
- 5 egg yolks
- 25 cl (8 fl oz) Yoplait crème fraîche
- 40 g (1½ oz) icing sugar

- Soak the gelatine in a little cold water. Press the raspberries through a mouli or fine sieve.
- Heat the milk with the vanilla pod.
- Beat the sugar with the egg yolks until thick and creamy; gradually whisk on the warm, flavoured milk, discarding the vanilla pod. Return the mixture to the saucepan and stir the custard over a moderate heat until it will coat the back of a spoon. Remove the custard from the heat. Add the drained gelatine and stir until dissolved. Pour through a fine sieve and leave to cool.
- Whip the crème fraîche with the icing sugar and fold into the cool custard; stir in the raspberry purée. Pour into a lightly oiled mould and chill for 4 hours.
- Unmould and serve with tiny orange biscuits.

Wine/Liqueur: A sparkling Framboise.

RASPBERRY AND PEACH GRATIN

Preparation: 20 minutes
Cooking: 20 minutes
Serves: 4

- 4 white fresh peaches
- 4 fresh yellow peaches
- 10 g (⅓ oz) caster sugar
- 1 sachet vanilla sugar*
- 2 egg yolks
- 15 cl (5 fl oz) Yoplait crème fraîche
- 15 g (½ oz) butter
- 300 g (10 oz) fresh raspberries

- Preheat the oven to 220°C (425°F, Gas Mark 7).
- Skin both varieties of peach; cut the flesh into quarters.
- Beat the sugars with the egg yolks and crème fraîche.
- Butter a gratin dish. Spread the peaches and raspberries in a layer and spoon the cream mixture evenly over the top. Bake in the oven for 20 minutes. Serve warm.

Wine: A Muscat de Beaumes-de-Venise.

* Sachets of vanilla-flavoured sugar are sold in health food shops and good grocers.

A SOUP OF RED FRUITS

Preparation: 20 minutes
Cooking: None
Chilling: 2 to 3 hours
Serves: 4

- 300 g (10 oz) fresh cherries
- 300 g (10 oz) fresh strawberries
- 400 g (14 oz) fresh raspberries
- 15 cl (5 fl oz) Yoplait crème fraîche
- 150 ml (5 fl oz) milk
- 50 g (1¾ oz) caster sugar
- sprigs fresh mint
- ice cubes

- Stone the cherries. Wash the strawberries and remove their stalky leaves; slice the strawberries.
- Place half the raspberries in the bowl of a food processor and blend until smooth; press through a fine sieve. Mix the sieved raspberry 'juice' with the crème fraîche, milk and sugar; chill for 2 to 3 hours.
- Just before serving, stir in the reserved raspberries, cherries and strawberries. Serve in bowls, with small sprigs of mint and an ice cube or two.

Wine: A very light but lively Beaujolais.

PEAR CHARLOTTE

Preparation: 1 hour
Marinating: 30 minutes
Cooking: 5 minutes
Chilling: 4 hours
Serves: 6

- 4 whole pears in syrup
- 100 ml (3½ fl oz) Poire William or other pear liqueur
- 4 leaves gelatine
- 500 ml (17 fl oz) milk
- vanilla pod
- 5 egg yolks
- 200 g (7 oz) caster sugar
- 10 cl (3½ fl oz) Yoplait crème fraîche
- 100 ml (3½ fl oz) iced water
- langues de chat biscuits

- Cut the pears into pieces; marinate in the Poire William for 30 minutes.
- Soak the gelatine in cold water.
- Heat the milk with the vanilla pod. Beat the egg yolks with the sugar until thick and creamy; gradually stir on the hot milk, a little a time, discarding the vanilla pod. Return the mixture to the saucepan and stir over a moderate heat until the custard will coat the back of a spoon.
- Turn the custard into a bowl and add the drained gelatine. Stir until dissolved and then pour through a fine sieve. Leave to cool.
- Place the crème fraîche and iced water in a chilled bowl; whisk until light and fluffy.
- Stir the drained pears into the cold custard.
- Dip the biscuits into the pear marinade and line the sides of a charlotte mould. Fold the whipped cream into the custard and turn the mixture into the mould; cover with more biscuits. Chill for 4 hours.
- Unmould and serve with a raspberry coulis.

Wine: Pineau des Charentes, the white variety.

PEAR AND APPLE TART

Preparation: 40 minutes
Cooking: 40 minutes
Serves: 6

• 3 pears
• 3 dessert apples
• 2 egg yolks
• 20 cl (6½ fl oz) Yoplait crème fraîche
• 2 pinches ground cinnamon
• 40 g (1½ oz) caster sugar
• 300 g (10 oz) shortcrust pastry

• Preheat the oven to 200°C (400°F, Gas Mark 6).
• Peel the pears and apples; remove the cores and cut into slices.
• Beat the egg yolks with the crème fraîche, cinnamon and sugar.
• Roll out the pastry fairly thinly and use to line a loose-bottomed flan tin, about 23 cm (9 inches) in diameter. Press up the edges well.
• Spread the sliced fruits over the pastry and pour the cream mixture carefully over the top. Bake in the oven for 40 minutes. Serve warm.

Liqueur: A glass of Calvados.

CREME BRULEE

Preparation: 1 hour
Cooking: 50 minutes
Chilling: 3 hours
Serves: 4

• 600 ml (1 pint) milk
• 4 sachets vanilla sugar*
• 10 egg yolks
• 150 g (5 oz) caster sugar
• 15 cl (5 fl oz) Yoplait crème fraîche
• 200 g (7 oz) soft brown sugar

• Place the milk and vanilla sugar in a heavy-based pan. Bring to the boil and then leave to cool.
• Preheat the oven to 160°C (325°F, Gas Mark 3).
• Beat the egg yolks with the caster sugar and crème fraîche; blend in the cooled, flavoured milk. Pour the mixture into a large gratin dish, or into individual ramekins. Stand in a roasting tin and add sufficient cold water to come halfway up the sides of the gratin dish or ramekins. Cook in the oven for 45 minutes.
• Remove the dishes, allow to cool and then chill for 3 hours.
• Scatter brown sugar generously over the top of the cream, and flash under a hot grill until caramelized. Serve immediately.

Wine: Muscat de Beaumes-de-Venise.

* Sachets of vanilla-flavoured sugar are sold in health food shops and good grocers.

CARAMEL ICE

Preparation: 40 minutes
Cooking: 20 minutes
Freezing: 4 hours
Serves: 4

- 1 litre (1¾ pints) Yoplait crème fraîche
- 500 ml (17 fl oz) cane sugar syrup
- 16 egg yolks
- 15 sugar cubes

- Place the crème fraîche and sugar syrup into a heavy-based pan; heat gently until just simmering.
- Beat the egg yolks briskly and carefully blend the warm crème fraîche on to them. Return the mixture to the pan and stir over a gentle heat until the mixture will coat the back of a spoon.
- In another small pan, dissolve the sugar lumps in 100 ml (3½ fl oz) water. Boil to a golden caramel. Blend the caramel into the custard mixture and leave to cool.
- Turn into an ice-cream maker and freeze.
- Serve in scoops with chocolate sauce.

Wine: Muscat de Rivesaltes.

VANILLA ICE

Preparation: 30 minutes
Cooking: 50 minutes
Freezing: 4 hours
Serves: 4

- 500 ml (17 fl oz) milk
- 2 vanilla pods
- 8 egg yolks
- 200 g (7 oz) caster sugar
- 30 cl (½ pint) Yoplait crème fraîche gastronomique

- Heat the milk with the vanilla pods. Beat the egg yolks with the sugar until pale and light. Stir on the milk, little by little, and return the mixture to the pan. Stir over a gentle heat until the custard will coat the back of a spoon; leave to cool.
- Discard the vanilla pods and mix the crème fraîche into the cold custard.
- Turn into an ice-cream maker and freeze.
- Serve in scoops with raspberry coulis.

Wine: Serve with a Crémant de Bourgogne.